Here & There

AA GILL

Here & There

collected travel writing

hardie grant books
MELBOURNE · LONDON

This book is fondly dedicated to my stepmother, Georgina Denison, whose ancestor built a small Martello tower in Sydney Harbour that still bears her name.

Contents

Introduction

Here and There wasn't my idea.

Here and There sounds a bit now and then, hot or cold, red or white, window or aisle. It's a bit hostess binary. I wanted to call it Aussie Tucker Walkabout, because that's the name of the file I keep these articles in. My little joke.

I told Pat, my editor at *Australian Gourmet Traveller*, that I wanted to call the collection Aussie Tucker Walkabout, and across a dozen time zones, 20 weather systems and 10,562 miles I could hear his eyeballs roll in their sockets. 'That's funny,' he said in the measured tone we keep for foreigners who copy our accents.

I'm lousy at titles. I've had bad reviews just for the titles of my books. And, actually, Here and There isn't bad. I'm here, you're there. Or perhaps you're here and I'm there. If there's anything that connects this collection of disparate and syncopated streams of peeved whimsy, then it is the hereness of there, and the thereness of here.

These are night-time thoughts, opinions and observations. They come out of the dark, are written last thing and filed to Australia as they or you start work, and I or they go to bed. I turn the lights out, check the locks and enjoy that peculiar, particular frisson of knowing that my chilly, damp words are now sunny, dry words; that a ten quid thought can emigrate to become a better idea, to be free and work hard and grow up to be a theory that it could never have been back here, or there. There's a sense of playing truant, a leave of absence in writing something for the next day, for people I don't really know, and better still, who don't know me. I have this alter ego now, this doppelganger.

One of the things that fascinates me about travelling is how places make people. The received travel writing wisdom is always the other way round: it's people who make places, who go out and carve nations from the rough, speechless, thoughtless wilderness. But over and over I'm aware that the characteristics and beliefs of nations seem to flow from the land, seep up from the earth.

It's not simply that people who live on plains are stoic and fatalistic and the people who live in mountains are intrepid and curious, or that island people are sybaritic and have naturally great abs, or that desert people, weirdly, never get lost. It's more complicated and subtle than that. National character, the collection of traits that make us different and therefore interesting, isn't random group consciousness or a collective serendipity. Tribal identities, from the taste for food to the love of the view to the sound of nursery rhymes to the jokes you laugh at, are peculiar to geography.

Australia is a good example. It has one of the most distinctive palettes of national identity on the globe, a way of being that is unmistakeably odd. People come from all over the globe to Australia, from ancient and robust cultures. But within months, sometimes within hours, they're transformed, made over into Australians. The land grabs them like God's own changing room. And I like to think that while I sleep here or there, down there, or up here, there is a wide-awake me in stubbies and thongs that is secretly living as an Australian.

Why do it?

It might not aid relaxation, or expand your mind, but travel will certainly give you blisters.

Why travel? I'm serious. What do you expect from somewhere else? Every parable, cautionary tale, every road movie comes to the conclusion that whatever it is you were looking for when you left was actually hidden in a biscuit tin in the spare room under a pillow, or was doing the washing up. People who travel to discover something, the wisdoms are generally agreed, are going the long way 'round to find it. The most annoying piece of portent-filled self-help you can be offered is the warning that however far you travel, you'll always find yourself there when you arrive.

The question 'why travel?' seems so obvious we rarely ask it. So much of our lives and income are spent planning and affording holidays. But what are we looking for? The travel industry spends a lot of time trying to figure out what we really want. Do you want this: the girl on the beach with the palm tree and the bendy hammock? Or this: the little terracotta fishing port with the lobster and the couple holding hands? In the end, travel agents generally agree that what most of you want is to pay less and go for longer.

But this simply presses the question: pay less and for longer of what? The most overused word in the travel industry is escape. Escape what? Travelling is time-out between two dimly clichéd places – a here that is fraught, hectic, relentless and infuriating, and a there that is peaceful, comforting, effortless and undemanding. But if that really describes your home and your holidays, then you're living your life the wrong way around.

So why do we go? Well, if you ask most people under 50, they simply go on holiday to go and get drunk and laid and tanned. Over 50, it's the pressing need to see and do things before you die. It's filling up the winged shopping trolley before the voice on the tannoy says this great round superstore and entertainment complex will be closing for you in six months. You don't want to be lying there on the waterproof sheet surrounded by people you don't recognise with the only thought in your head being, damn, I wish I'd seen the Taj Mahal. (By the way, if you're over 60 and you haven't seen the Taj, drop everything. Do it now.)

The great PR lie of travel is that it broadens your mind. Go and ask that illegal immigrant folding the towels in your tennis club if the extraordinarily circuitous journey he made to get to carry your bag broadened his mind. Ask what one-worldly insights the middle-management drone who has to fly to Brisbane, Singapore and Frankfurt once a month gets. Travel doesn't necessarily make you wiser, nicer, better tempered, more open or calmer. If you travel a lot it makes you well travelled. And that's something.

Of all the dumbest reasons for travel, the most thoughtless expectation of a holiday is to relax. Just going to vegetate for a couple of weeks, you've bought some trashy novels and some SPF-30, and you're going to just turn into a softly poached egg by the pool? Well how did checking-in to an international airport, a long-haul flight, checking-out of a Third-World international airport (twice: there and back), changing money, dealing with people

who are a thousand times poorer than you in a foreign
language without being rude or patronising, not being able
to drink the water or eat the vegetables, having to take
malaria pills, cholera, yellow fever and meningitis and
polio injections – how did all that ever get to be the raw
ingredients for just chilling out? If you want to relax, go to
bed. Draw the curtains. Watch golf.

Travelling to do nothing is the great holiday oxymoron,
but it's still a growing part of the industry. There is no
corner of the world where you won't find a spa with a
pedicurist and a Thai girl behind the desk telling you that
all the massages are booked up until Friday. Mind you,
one of the most extraordinary men I ever came across was
in a spa. It was in Addis Ababa, of all places. Addis is
not by a yoga stretch of anyone's imagination a relaxing
place. It's utterly fascinating. Ethiopia is possibly the
most singular place in the world. Certainly it stands apart
in Africa as being kin only to itself. Addis is quite an
angry place, or at least it was when I was there for Haile
Selassie's funeral. In the Mercato, the largest market
on the continent, there are enough vampire-eyed khat
addicts, secret policemen, ex-torturers, trainee kidnappers
and poor, bored youths to make strolling around
touristically, even in broad daylight, a risky activity.
Ethiopia is home to some of the most gallantly vicious and
uncompromisingly psychopathic warriors in the world.
They don't offer you a big Caribbean welcome. That's not
to say that they're unfriendly; they just don't decide they
like you before they know you, or because you're foreign.

Rising out of the middle of some of the most hopeless
slums you could ever wish to see is a mammoth Mordor
of a luxury hotel. The real deal, not the usual African
four-star deluxe. Here, everything worked, or did; the

aircon, the phones, the lift, the waiters. There was ice, and everything on the menu was available. It was weirdly astonishing, apparently built with Gulf money for the Gulf appetite for the most elegantly beautiful women in the world.

You could have a massage by the pool, and there was this old man, really old, with long, elegant hands and fingers that were bony and strong, but absolutely assured. They moved about like a troop of slim, burrowing rodents. He was completely blind, had been born blind. Haile Selassie had invented a school for blind children to teach them how to be masseurs. It's the sort of thing that utter dictators can do on a whim, and it's sort of brilliant. They were the finest, most sensitive masseurs in the world, and this was the last, the last blind masseur in Africa.

He had felt interesting times – revolutions, terror, famine, death – all through the bodies of the men who'd caused it, and he had a remarkable gift. My girlfriend went to him and he asked her where she was from. London, she replied. No – he held her foot – you've come home. You're from Africa. And although you couldn't tell to hear her, she is indeed from Durban. And then, with a firm curiosity, he travelled his fingers over the soles of her feet, and told her every country she'd walked in, never making a mistake, never getting one wrong.

Our feet have a diary, a passport. We keep a physical journal of the lands we've trod. I'm not making any of this up; it's not a traveller's tale. And there's a moral here. Travel doesn't broaden the mind, but it does give you interesting blisters.

The market-driven truth

A market reflects the people it serves — what they have, what they need — except in France, where they're for worshipping, not shopping.

My weakness, my pleasure, is markets. Whenever they say, what would you like to see? The museum, the opera house, the red light district, the bridge over the river? I always say the market. I want to see where the women buy their vegetables. I want to see the fish, the butchers, the quarter of cobblers and tailors. You can't fake a market. You can't make it what it's not. It is as true a reflection of the people it serves as anything; what they have, don't have, what they make and import, and what their pretensions and weaknesses are.

The Mercato in Addis Ababa, biggest market in Africa: dangerous red-eyed tribesmen, maddened and delusional on khat, unloading bushels of the stuff flown in daily from the ancient cities on the Somali border. The stalls selling coffee and the winding lanes of incense dealers, the gifts of the Magi, smelling of martyrdom and plainsong.

Tsukiji, the Tokyo fish market: miles of frozen tuna, lying like a thousand unexploded bombs steaming in the dawn as the auctioneers paint red characters on them, buyers cutting tiny nuggets of flesh from their tails to knead for water content. The unspeakable nameless

---

denizens of a dozen oceans flapping and squirming
in brine, all the height of gustatory sophistication, or
speechlessly depressing, depending on where you stand.

The fish market in Zanzibar: a slithery soup of scales
and guts and too-few fish, the spindly outrigged dhows
having to go further and further into the Indian Ocean
to find a catch. And then the fish markets of southern
Spain, where everything is kept alive, the skate laid on
their backs with their squashed baby faces, dribbling
blood from their severed tails, looking like mortifyingly
religious parables.

The dawn markets in Saigon: vast and frantic, but
beautiful. Thousands of ducks and chickens waiting to
be plucked, mountains of flowers. The Grand Bazaar of
Istanbul, with its streets of gold-dealers and ziggurats of
pastel Turkish delight, the caviar merchants, the bags
of nuts and dried fruit. Peshawar's many, many markets:
older than civilisation, leatherworkers making bandoliers
and sandals with the soles of old Russian tyres, the
pomegranate-juice sellers, and the boys trussing and
skewering sparrows.

Crawford Market in Bombay, the book market in
Calcutta, the bird market in Denpasar, the karaoke
market in Tashkent. All markets are vitally and vibrantly
different, but they're also fundamentally similar. They
work on the universal principles of supply and demand,
daily bread, bargains, extravagance and thrift. Markets are
the true face of cities and of countries.

But of all the markets in the world, there is one
example that stands as a template for markets – the
market's market, the perfect market against which all
others are measured: the weekly markets of southern
France. Most white, Western, middle-aged tourists travel

to France in the belief that here they will find the apogee of domestic sophistication and taste. Apart from all the hot and tedious haute couture, the museums, the churches, the ruins and the endless, endless art, which must of course be genuflected to and murmured at reverentially, the true civilised genius of France is not what it has made and done, but what it doesn't do. And not doing anything, with a languid haughtiness, is France's great contribution to the Western canon.

The great places of pilgrimage for masterly inactivity are France's markets. The markets entrance and astonish and comfort the rest of the world because somehow they manage to encompass and impart a way of life that is particularly, peculiarly French. No one outside France has quite managed to codify or explain cogently what this uniquely French existence consists of, so they come up with a French phrase to encompass it all: *je ne sais quoi.*

Je ne sais quoi is France's abiding gift to the world. More *je ne sais quoi* for your euro is to be found in a French market than anywhere else. We wander down the aisles of trestles and stalls aghast at the marvellous repose of produce. There are peaches warm from the tree, ripe and golden. Figs, green and black, bursting with sweet, ancient, darkly lascivious simile. The smell of fresh lemon, the bunches of thyme and lavender and verbena, the selections of oil and olives, pale green and pungent, and the honey, from orange blossom, from heath and orchard, and the beeswax. The charcuterie, the dozens of ancient and dextrous things to do with a dead pig, in all the hues of pink and pale, fatty cream.

The smell of the complements of pimiento and fennel, the strings of sausages, of bones, of pâté and rillettes. And then there's the ducks, with their unctuous, giving, bloated, lustrous livers, poached in sealed jars cuddled around truffles and cognac. And pirouetting chickens, like coutured birds smelling of very heaven with delicate legs poised on a spit. The boulanger, with loaves crisp and hard, plaited and rounded, wheat and rye, malted and dusted. Bitter crusts and soft sour centres, the pastries and sweetmeats, the plates and bowls of little titbits in sauce, the oeufs en gelée, the asparagus, the snails with their puffy green butter stuffing, the store selling napery and embroidery, the beautiful rustic starched pride of peasant tables and French rooms. The fussy caps for confitures and cake trays, the chocolatiers with their outré soft-centres, and the cheeses – the land of a thousand cheeses. The market will wind its way around a boules-rabbled square with pollarded planes and uncomfortable ironwork benches, and at its corners will be the most holy of holies in the *je ne sais quoi* market: a café. A café with cream and pink woven chairs and little metal tables and a waiter with a long apron and the look of a man who is beaten by his wife. And here you will meet the rest of your party after two hours of worshipping at the long temple of Frenchness and order your café au lait and perhaps just an Armagnac, if you're having one, and perhaps a tasse of the rough but immensely agreeable local wine – just to smell it is to understand utterly the superiority of terroir over mere talent.

And you can examine the rewards of your forage, the amulets of pilgrimage. Oh, I didn't get much – just this artichoke, because I liked the colour. Oh well, we got this marvellous chèvre. The man said it was made with his grandmother's goats, or perhaps that his grandmother was a goat. And this charming gingham bag for hanging on the back of the kitchen door and keeping old plastic bags in.

Not, of course, that we now use plastic bags anymore, on principle. And no, you're right – we don't actually have a kitchen door, either. But still, it seemed so here, so right. I'll give it to the daily; she's from the Philippines. Did anyone get any olives? I tried to get some of that divine-looking pâté, but I think I bought an eggtimer instead.

And here is the truth of French markets: it's almost impossible to actually buy anything in them. If you had to really do your entire weekly shop in one, it would take you a fortnight. So consequently the French don't – they use supermarkets like everyone else. This isn't for buying, it's for worshipping. France isn't really like this at all, it's just an idea of a France just like this. This is where they teach their *je ne sais quoi* before they go to the convenience store, the gym and the office and figure out how to be more like the Germans and the English and the Irish and the Americans. I said that what I liked about markets was that you couldn't fake them, that they're immutably driven by commerce. Except for these ones. They are the exception that proves the rule. The French are not like their markets at all. Their markets are actually like the rest of us, or our ideal selves. Somebody once said that when good Americans die they go to Paris. Well, the rest of us go to a market somewhere in the south of France.

All in the family

*Only in Sicily is organised crime
a tourist attraction. Just don't
ask the locals about it.*

There are many singular and specific things about Sicily.
Indeed, Sicily is a specifically singular place. But perhaps
the most striking singular thing is that it's the only holiday
destination on earth that tourists visit because of the
organised crime. Sicily has the distinction, dubious or
ironic, of having murderous kidnapping and extortion as
an attraction, like the whirling dervishes of Istanbul or the
street mimes of Vienna. (Actually, slightly less murderous
than the street mimes of Vienna.)

The mafia's USP – and I think in this it is also alone
in the world of crime – is having a strict rulebook that
prohibits the robbing of strangers. You keep it in the
family. Sicilians are understandably taciturn and annoyed
by the visitors' interest in their thugs. It's like having
a psychopath in the family that everyone else thinks is
a charming and exciting raconteur. The black hand of
crime families grew out of the grotesque feudal poverty
of the Bourbon rule of Sicily. Peàsants had no rights, no
redress and no justice; the secret organisation grew from
the aching tumour of revenge. But unlike Robin Hood,
the mafia didn't rob from the rich to give to the poor; it
robbed the poor and protected the poor against robbery,
setting up a circular monopoly of both crime and crime
prevention that has lasted ever since. Taxi drivers and

hotel concierges fend off the inquisitive questions from tourists with a wearied thin politeness, like men being asked about their prostates.

From the moment you land in Palermo, you're aware that one of the defining characteristics of Sicily is that it isn't like the rest of Italy. A secretive, watchful, hard and self-contained place, there is none of the light-hearted bantering and flirtation you associate with the mainland. Indeed, there are few women around, and it's outwardly as overtly masculine as the countries across the straits in North Africa. I was always aware of being watched in the hugger-mugger collapsing streets of the old capital. Whenever I looked over my shoulder there was somebody looking back. Not threatening or intimidating, just noticing, marking your movements through the teeming streets. The balconies of the old baroque houses have blankets hung over their metal balustrades to protect the modesty of daughters leaning over to whisper secrets and dart dark, meaningful glances. Or just hang out the washing.

There are hundreds of huge and vainglorious palaces here, ancient and decrepit, dropping their decoration and pediment like stone lepers. They're blackened and crippled, strung with utility cables like life-support, and inside the warren of rooms is a mass of illegal immigrants from Tunisia and points south from Africa. The poignancy and beauty of extreme penury and desperation set against crumbling, reduced grandeur is one of the endearing pleasures of sightseeing. Picturesque slums were ever the background of The Grand Tour, which took in Sicily for the poorest and most aesthetically pleasing peasants in Europe. Its ruins of half-a-dozen defunct civilisations and Mount Etna continue to be the living symbols of hubris and nemesis: compared to the power of ancient gods, human vanity and aesthetics are merely laughable graffiti.

There are few places that have quite so much naked, molten history as Sicily. Dozens of invasions, uncountable massacres and clearances, relentless vendettas. The past infects the present and the future, it glows in the brooding, and seeps from one generation to the next. Blood, as they say around here, calls for blood. Everything about Sicily seems to be a cautionary tale. Everything is itself and a symbol and part of a code. It's not an easy place to grasp, or necessarily one that you're drawn to. There are a lot of people here, a lot of poor people and a lot of corruption. Modern buildings of the most dispiriting type seen outside the dreams of Stalinism crust every hillside and elbow every small town. There was a time in the '70s when they said Sicily was the second-biggest importer of concrete in the world after Nigeria. It was a society adept at milking the guilt and hush-money of European grants for the least lasting good.

But it still manages a striking and harsh beauty, an unpolished or unfenced sense of the ages made palpable and accessible. A people whose hardship and secrets have also given surprising moments of sweetness and sympathy. I was particularly drawn to the confectionery. Traditionally cakes and pastries are made by nuns in closed and silent orders, who make delicate and intricate moments of almond and honey with infusions of soft fruit and citrus and chestnut, sugared and shaped into devout little braille prayers. There are hundreds of these sweet things offered to martyrs or on religious holidays. The intensity and the hardness of the belief and the life made them give each a flavour that transcends the marzipan and ricotta. They have a memory of the crypt, a veiled reminder of incense and death. And behind the childish pleasure of sweetness is mortality and pain and guilt and mortification. The island is heavy with mandarin oranges. The air is full of the smell of their blossom, heady and morbid.

I went up to the small hill village of Savoca in the south-west. Not many people make it up here. It's a typical Sicilian village, buttoned down and shuttered. It curls in on itself like a stone snake with an itch. There's a good church, which is locked, with an interesting Norman mural, a crypt of dried mummies with bay leaves and rags in their stomachs, and a view that stretches across the centuries to the sea.

'Wait for me 'round the corner,' said the Sicilian I was working with. 'There's a bar, you may know it. They made that film there.' And indeed I did know it. This is the bar from *The Godfather*, where Michael meets the girl that he will briefly marry. It's one of the great scenes, one of the great locations, in all of the short history of movies. Coppola used it to stand in for Corleone, a real place with long mafia associations but which has become too modern.

Film tourism has now become big business, and I sat in the park opposite, where Michael had his wedding reception, and wondered why there was not a single intimation of what this place had once briefly been. My friend found me. 'Do you recognise it?' he asked.

'Yes, it's exactly the way it is in the film, isn't it?'

'Oh, I don't know,' he said. 'I haven't seen it.'

'You haven't seen *The Godfather*? Everyone's seen *The Godfather*.'

'Not in Sicily,' he said. 'Why would we?'

Battle of the bulge

Budgie-smugglers, apple-catchers ... call them what you will, there's no doubting there are strong cultural ties that bind us to our more extreme swimwear choices.

I spent my first holiday in Spain for years. Andalusia. I'd forgotten what a vast business holidays are here. What Seattle is to computers, Bangladesh is to T-shirts, and Guangzhou is to small plastic toy cars with cartoon drivers, so Spain is to getting your bits burnt. Spain invented tourism. Obviously people had to go places before Spain came up with sea, sun, sex and sangria, but tourists tended to do what it said on the package: they toured. They went to look at things. Tourism was cities and ruins and self-improvement, not snoggery.

It was the Spanish who had the uncharacteristically blue-sky idea of taking the interest out of travel, of removing the place from the destination. At the moment when aeroplanes got to their destinations more often than they disappeared into oceans, and working people thought it was safe enough and cheap enough to go away for a couple of weeks abroad instead of staying in Torquay or Bournemouth, the Spanish realised that the one thing that had been putting most Europeans off being tourists was the touring bit, the self-improvement, the churches

and the ruins and the guide with the raised umbrella
saying, 'This way please – we have half an hour to do
six centuries of frescoes, so no talking.' The Spanish
brilliantly discerned that what really attracted people was
each other. The dons heard a mysterious disembodied
voice saying, 'Build it and they will come.' (He probably
said it in Spanish.)

So they built Malága, and come they did, in their
hundreds of thousands. They came because of the sun,
and the bit of water, and the cheap wine and the paella,
but mostly just for the sun. And the Spanish also realised
that if the tourists wanted to go and see something exciting
or edifying, then they'd just look at each other. And it
turned out that most people would far rather look at each
other than some old statue without arms. And to those who
pointed out that they could have stayed home and looked
at each other on the bus, the answer was plain: not in this
colour, and certainly not wearing that. Where else could
you see that particular swatch of human colouring range
from deep-flayed puce to wizened-sideboard teak, and
wearing such spectacular attention-seeking clobber?

It is no accident that both the British and the Germans
so often find themselves rubbing peeling shoulders as
guests of the incredulous Spanish. The Poms and the
Krauts are the two most dowdy dressers at home, but when
it comes to packing for the summer, then some pantomime
switch is flicked on in their heads, some exhibitionist
pheromone perhaps contained in suntan cream. The
astonishing ability to throw caution, taste, sense and
decorum to the breeze is particularly strong in both the
Germans and the British.

It has always been a matter of mutually fond
embarrassment, but now something has happened on the

beaches and lidos and swimming pools of Europe, and of course it's been precipitated by the French, who are people who wear more casual clothes on holiday than they do formal ones at funerals. Nobody looks quite as uncomfortably creased, polished and preened as a French man trying to look relaxed. A French woman has just been turned away from the municipal swimming pool dressed in what they're calling a burqini, which is essentially all her clothes and a headscarf. This is the accepted sharia outfit for mixed bathing. The pool guard turned her away for being unhygienic, a swimming hazard, unfavourable and a fashion disaster. At the same time, it transpires that it is illegal in France for men to approach swimming pools unless they're wearing Speedos. The shorts that most of us wear are apparently unhygienic. In response, an English holiday camp has banned Speedos. Europe is now bristling and pouting and posing its particular pet intolerances about what you should wear to go swimming.

A tracksuit with three headscarves is a bit of a red herring, or perhaps a shoal of kippers. If you're that modest, most women don't want to swim with men at all. The Speedo thing, though, is interesting. The bits of Europe where they're still popular generally coincide with places that still elect Communist mayors, where the most popular occupation for women is either housewife or prostitute, and where the local drink is made out of distilled plums or potatoes. So very tight budgie-smugglers, as I think the Australians call them, being the home of budgies, or apple-catchers, as they're known in England, are generally popular all the way down the Black Sea, on the right-hand side of the Adriatic, and on the south side of the Baltic. So it's Ukranians, Serbs, Romanians and Bulgarians, and very, very small costumes

are very, very big in Albania and in Hungarian spas.
Germans, of course, adore them and always have. They
wear them wherever possible. The Brits, the Italians and
of course the Americans wouldn't be seen dead in nylon
girl pants. As far as I remember, Australia is pretty much
split down the middle. A lot of them wear very baggy
board shorts, but there's also quite a lot of muscle Marys
in lifeguard-style tanga.

The point of this argument in Europe is, like most
arguments in Europe, not about what it says it's about.
It isn't about swimming trunks. It's about comparing
versions of liberal intolerance. So the French banned
women in burqinis because it's an insult to women.
Muslims complain it's intolerant of faith. The Brits banned
budgie-smugglers because they're offensive to women and
children. Very brown Polish men say it's an infringement
of their right to wear whatever they like. And actually
we're having this row because we're so fed up with and
frightened about having to argue about the things that
really matter, like unemployment and house repossessions.

What no one has yet asked is: what's worse in Speedos?
A very little one, or a very big one? I mean, if your
budgie-smugglers contain, say, a day-old chick or a
cockatoo, which is worse?

What's also interesting about Europe at the moment
is that naturism is declining. Its particular sexless,
healthy and rather dull image of hiking and caravans
and woodland clearings is disappearing under a new
Puritanism and the fear of paedophilia and sexual
impropriety. The French, also, contrarily, have given up
going topless on the beach. Again, this Bardot-esque
symbol of equality and freedom has been usurped by
so many plastic breasts and Ukranian students on the

Riviera. It's been a weirdly Calvinist summer here.
Europe's existential chickens have come home to roost.
Or perhaps that's budgies, or maybe cockatoos, or
kookaburras, and the occasional albatross.

Food for thought

- -

*With the rapid devolution of
fast food and the Darwinian
drive of bastardised dishes
around the globe, croissants and
cappuccinos just aren't what
they used to be.*

I just went out to have coffee. Normally I just go to the
kitchen to have coffee, but today there are two Poles in
the kitchen, and if I have to make coffee for me, then
I've got to make it for them, too, which would involve the
international mime of beverage-making, and searching
under dust sheets for the fridge and biscuits. Poles, I've
discovered, are quite fussy about biscuits, so I went out.
I always associate going out for coffee in the morning with
New York. It's a ritual lots of American writers have: you
take your *Times* and the *Post* and you do coffee. Some take
their computers and sit in Starbucks and work. There's
a whole school of Starbucks journalism, movies and
television, all frothy profundity and witty banter. A chance
romantic meeting between two writers, one serious (her),
the other sporty and not serious (him), in a coffee shop is
the leitmotif of the Starbucks school.

So I went down the road and had a cappuccino. Like
eggs Benedict and unhygienic sex, it's one of those
things that received wisdom says you never get at home.
Everybody has a cappuccino thing, but whoever uses them

twice? It takes hours, it coats the ceiling in watery milk, and finally you get cold coffee with scum. I rarely drink cappuccino. The waitress asked if I'd like a croissant (she was Polish, incidentally; Britain is now run entirely by Poles, and frankly they're doing a far better job than any of the other people who have invaded us for the last 2000 years) and I said yes. I said yes because there is an old connection. We think of cappuccino as Italian and croissants as French, but actually they're both Austrian. Precisely, they both originate with the siege of Vienna, which was the high water-mark of the Turkoman invasion of Europe, and the beginning of the slow withering of Ottoman expansion. The croissant was made to celebrate the defeat of Islam by a grateful Viennese baker; it still comes under the heading of Viennoiserie in France. The coffee was discovered in a Turkish camp and mixed with milk and named after the monks in white hoods. They have since gone around the world.

I expect a cappuccino and a croissant are the two things you can pretty much get in every country on the globe. Mine came and the coffee was a pneumatic effluvium, not unlike cavity wall insulation. It was striped like a zebra's bandage with a thick layer of cocoa. Finding the actual coffee in it was a trepidatious business; at last a grey liquid seeped from below. It was mildly coffee-flavoured warm milk. But the croissant was the real surprise. A lump covered in almonds and a shake of icing sugar that mice could've skied on, it was a fat, corpulent thing, like a croissant python that had swallowed a doughnut. As I tried to pick it up, it fell apart under its own adipose cholesterolic weight, spilling its guts of a slidey mousse made of fat and ground almonds and sugar, like a six-year-old's cake mix. Together the coffee and the cake were to their original inspirations what a pantomime dame is to Elle Macpherson. It isn't that they were horrible. It's that they had descended so far from their template.

I spent 10 minutes just watching them, half expecting that they might continue to metamorphose on the counter, slowly becoming a united sweet sludge. And I began to think about the worldwide eugenics of food. There is a set of international dishes that have shed their national origins and, like rats, pigeons, fleas and boy bands, become ubiquitous. Freed from the scrutiny of their families, they grow degenerate, spoilt, sloppy, lascivious, foul-mouthed, inconsistent, amoral, slovenly bits of mouthy comfort.

Take pizza. It started as a simple ascetic crisp stretch of dough, frugally flavoured with tomato and mozzarella, perhaps with the addition of a sliver of local ham, a sprig of rosemary. Away from Naples, into the fleshpots, it became a bloated painted whore. Anything can have a go on a deep-crust pizza, and anything does: pineapple, caviar, smoked salmon, cheddar. It's been cosmetically enhanced and coarsened. And Caesar salad – a simple and clever piece of serendipity that married cos lettuce, egg, parmesan, garlic, anchovies and croutons – has grown into a soppy cold stew of chicken and bacon, smothered in mayonnaise, invariably without anchovy.

The list of things that grow wayward when they leave home is the longest lamented menu in the world. From dim sum to chicken tikka, there is a Darwinian natural selection in these fast food international dishes. Re-created without chefs, unencumbered by recipes, often with their constituent parts, their DNA, mass-produced by technicians with degrees in engineering, this is food that has become its own master, and to survive in the competitive stuff-throat world of cheap catering, it has to adapt to attract the humans who are needed to consume it as part of its natural life cycle.

We all think that when we pick up a menu we are the predators, we are the hunters, the grazers and browsers, but have you ever considered that you are in fact also the prey, that the hamburger needs you quite as much as you desire it? The memory of its taste, its coarse smell, the dribble of nameless juices, is what it uses to lure you in. Without millions of victims worldwide, the hamburger would go the way of the Cornish pasty, the posset, salmagundi, sops; the list of extinct dishes is quite as long as the list of wayward ones, a list of extinct dishes that couldn't adapt to colonise new palates and markets.

I sat looking at my cappuccino and croissant and considered that in their instigation these two simple things represented a triumph, not just of the West against the invading hordes, but of taste and culture, craft and civilisation. The delicate lightness of the croissant with its wonderful chewy heart, the coffee the result of a combination of trade and discovery from Africa, Arabia and Europe, a synthesis of curiosities, each to start every new morning. In their inception, they were the best of us. In their mass production, their sweet, unctuous, stupid, slurred, caloried, careless flavours, their toothless textures, they appeal to the worst of us. There is, in the descent of fast global grub, a moral, and also a warning: who do you think is consuming who?

Bombay dreams

Ultimate enlightenment lies in the collective will, intelligence and glamour of civilisation, and the bustling city of Bombay is the perfect place to find it.

Travellers can be divided into two categories: those who travel to get away from people, and those who travel to find people. The fashionable thing now is to go to a place where there is no one. For some unfathomable reason, it's called ecotourism. Places that don't have people in them generally don't have people in them for a reason. The Norwegian government is offering cheap flights to the extreme north of the country, just shy of the North Pole, with the teasing promise that 'it's the most remote place on earth'. Except, of course, for the airport and the plane full of gym instructors, camping-shop fantasists, extreme vegans and travel bloggers you'll find there, all shivering blissfully in the blinkered belief that they're on their own learning something pristine and magically true about themselves and the world. Well, I've been to the Arctic Circle, and I can tell you, if you can find somewhere so remote that Eskimos won't live there, then you've got about half an hour to get somewhere they do.

The first travel piece I wrote was about the salt pans in the Kalahari – still one of my favourite places on earth. Nothing lives there. Birds don't fly, fish don't swim, antelope don't stot (that, by the way, is a technical term for what antelopes do; they also 'pronk'). Whatever stots, pronks, saunters, limps or flaps into the Makgadikgadi stays there and desiccates. I came across a man who had a New-Age revelation in the Kalahari. He was a rather ordinary buttoned-up mercantile chap. He told me he'd taken his spade and wandered into the bright, glittering nothingness for his morning ablution and, while squatting in the unforgiving spotlight with naught for his modesty, he was blinded by the truth that he was merely a speck in the great spinning harmony of the spheres. Stripped away of everything, including his dignity, he understood that he was a small thing. And? I asked. And what? he said. And, what else? Nothing else. He grew quite peeved: Isn't that enough, the cosmic truth that we are just dust in the Hoover-bag of existence? Well, that's not so much a revelation as a French cartoon cliché. How dare you call my revelation a cliché? Don't you know who I am?

And that's rather the point of New-Age travel into wildernesses. It leads to a pompous snobbery – the wisdom that belongs to those who have been to the high places and the distant shores, and it's all a nonsense and a delusion. The idea that there is some kind of special found knowledge, some higher understanding indebted to nature, is quite a modern one. It was invented in the 18th century by the Romantics and was centred prosaically around the manicured crags of Switzerland and the sodden sod of the Lake District. Wordsworth and Byron and various composers and lady watercolourists found an awe in the outdoors, and they commandeered a new word for it: they called it the sublime. Beauty, you see, was a man-made thing. The sublime was what was created by wind, rain, time and the god of your choice. And, in it, they found a great metaphor for people with too much time on their hands, too many black suits and too little sex.

The other type of traveller, the one in whose caravanserai I happily include myself, is after people and the places of people. We are the older school. We trace our tour guides back to Herodotus, and they include Marco Polo, Richard Burton, Moses and Genghis Khan. We understand that the greatest wonders of the world are all man-made and they're wonders because men made them. That what's ultimately enlightening is the collective will, intelligence, aesthetics, fun and glamour of civilisation. So this piece is belatedly about one of the greatest cities in the world, Bombay. (We don't say Mumbai. Only newsreaders and charity workers say Mumbai.)

Bombay is a city where it's impossible to avoid people. Indeed, the defining grace and glory of the whole subcontinent is its people. The teeming, steaming great masterpiece of humanity. Every vista, every angle has a cast of thousands, and Bombay is one of its principal joys. It's not a beautiful city, not in the man-made sense, not in the Venice or Prague sense, although it has many spectacular parts. Its attraction lies in the throb and the hum of its population. It is a city in the process of shedding its skins. It was the great port of Empire, a self-consciously provincial view of the East from Home Counties clerks, a place of order and self-conscious provincial good taste. Victoria Station is an absurd totem of stiff grandeur to English self-regard and smug grandiloquence. Crawford Market is an attempt to turn a bazaar into a department store, with decoration and a fountain designed by Rudyard Kipling's father. Kipling was born nearby, in the art school. And when the British left, Bombay reverted to being a city of Parsee

mercantile wealth, and Indian snobbery. Then along came
Bollywood, and it got a whole lot sexier. Now it's got music
and advertising and banking and financial services and
a middle class that has reached some sort of delicate
tipping point against the teeming penury. It is a city that
is glowing with energy. It is a mesmerising attraction for
India's rural poor, who arrive in their thousands every
day to camp in packing cases, a ghost city that fills in
the gaps between the real concrete-and-glass city like
human ivy. They're here for the chance to be part of it,
to jump aboard the spinning generator of light, power,
wealth and discontent.

None of these are reasons you'd generally go to visit a
city. As a rule, we visit metropolises that were once great
but have now settled into old age, a charming decrepitude,
so that we view the spoils of enthusiasm as nostalgia.
But you really should go and see Bombay. This is a city
becoming, shrugging off its past and bursting into the
future. It's riveting and enthusing just to be stuck in its
traffic jams for a few days.

And if you want to get a head-full of the sublimity of
humanity, then come and look at Bombay as a natural
wonder, a human Niagara, a rainforest of CVs, a Grand
Canyon of ambition. And if that's not enough, then
there's the best street food in India. And if you want to
shop, there's the finest shopping in India, including the
marvellous antiques market on Mutton Street. There's a
sophisticated nightlife that's as expensive as Tokyo and
as sexy as Rome. There's cricket at the weekends played
against a backdrop of colonial Gothic steeples. And there's
life, pulsating and grasping and dreaming with great
politeness and vanity. If you're fed up with being made to
feel guilty for being born human, then go to Bombay and

be reminded what a brilliant, breathtaking species we are. In the end, that's the distinction between those who travel to see nature and those who travel to see people. The one is ultimately all about you. The other is all about everyone else. Wilderness travellers are self-regarding bores. Humanity-commuters are the storytellers.

Call of the wild

On big-game hunts in the African wilderness, there is a tangible sense of being part of the rough and violent scheme of nature.

Africa is the great divide for many travellers. For the worldly, Africa contains more places that they don't want to go to and more things that they don't want to see than anywhere else in the solar system. I suspect you could divide the globe into two groups: those who wake up every morning thinking, 'Thank God I'm not in Africa,' and those who look out of the window first thing and think, 'What I wouldn't give to be in Africa.' Admittedly, the second group is a whole lot smaller than the first. I know because I'm one of them. And like the members of some geo-religious sect, we fall upon each other's necks when we meet because most of the time we're having to explain to the incredulous and the repulsed what we like about the Dark Continent.

There is a third group: those who wake up and say, 'Oh my God, get me out of Africa.' I know that however frightening, threatening and distasteful it can be to visit Africa, it's nothing on how tough it must be to live there. Of all the seven continents, Africa has the worst reputation. Ever since my first visit 25 years ago, I've missed it. A year without a trip to Africa is a year without a particular flavour of heat, sense of colour. And this year, although I'd been to Algeria, I'd not set foot in black

Africa. It didn't look like it was going to happen, and
then a friend said, 'Why don't you come and join me in
the bush in northern Tanzania for a week?' and I bought
a ticket there and then. And my heart sang, and my soul
quivered, and my doctor started filling prescriptions
and needles. One of the most embarrassing and shaming
things about going to Africa is that we have to take an
expensive chunk of First-World pharmacopoeia with us.
Prophylactics, inoculations, oils, ointments, unctions and
sprays, none of which are available or offered to people
who live there.

I had been invited to go big-game hunting, in the bush
that runs along the southern edge of the Serengeti plain
and the Ngorongoro Crater. I'd never done this before.
I don't have a problem with hunting per se – I spent quite
a lot of my autumn shooting birds and stalking deer –
but game hunting in Africa comes with a long tail: from
Teddy Roosevelt to Ernest Hemingway and all those army
officers galloping about bagging things, and the murderous
taxidermically challenged Americans, looking for big and
rare things to decapitate in the name of interior decoration.

If you peruse YouTube, you'll find that the very
cream of all of the most objectionable white males in the
universe are posting little films of themselves wearing
absurd amounts of camouflage over their paunches and
baseball caps, dribbling over mega-ammunition and rifles
that would cost five years' wages of the men who have
to carry them. These hunters beam on raw mainlined
adrenaline, punching the air over some diminished corpse.
It's not a good look, and it's not something I want to be
associated with.

But then, being white in Africa comes with all sorts of
bad looks. Every white face arrives trailing a long story.

And that's difficult, and you wish that you could wear a T-shirt that read, 'Really, I'm not like all the others', in 13 tribal languages. But of course you are.

I'd never done big-game hunting, and I was interested particularly because I like being out in the bush, and this was a couple of weeks before the rains were due. The temperatures were stifling. Everything was parched into shades of beige and terracotta, but there were still amazing splashes of green, and in the brittle grass, flame-ball lilies of bright orange and yellow sprouted miraculously.

If you didn't know, you'd think all this was a dying place, that precious little would return from the desiccation. Every afternoon the heat rises, and the great cumulonimbus clouds sit on the horizon like mountain ranges, a threat and a promise of things to come. This is not beautiful in any traditional aesthetic way. This land has got more forms than any other living environment. Everything is gnarled and bent, hunched and defensive. Everything has to fight for its little corner. It's like looking at nature with all the adjectives stripped away.

This is where we came to hunt buffalo. Buffalo are mythologised by hunters as the most frightening animal in Africa. They're not. It's the ones with the guns that are most frightening. But buffalo are huge and tend to be bad tempered. They have short sight but excellent hearing and noses, and will charge first and ask questions later. (They don't ask very complicated questions.) They are very unpredictable when threatened or spooked. Most herd animals will run. Running offers the best statistical option for every individual in the herd. However, in small groups, ones or twos, it can be that attack offers the best statistical option, so buffalo can go either way.

A professional hunter, two local trackers and I stalked
into the middle of herds of buffalo, waiting beside trees,
standing very still, like big kids in silly hats playing
Grandmother's Footsteps or What's the Time Mister Wolf,
as the huge black cows slowly moved past us, sniffing the
air, staring with small, baggy eyes, sensing something.
Watching buffalo is spectacular. In fact, I can't think
of any other 40 minutes of my life that have been as
completely concentrated on one task. Every footfall
and every movement becomes as precise as a mime
in a graveyard, becomes slowed down, becomes hyper-
real. You're aware of the tiniest details, every noise,
every small insect. Finally, the shot is just a point in
a paragraph.

It is awkward, through the fork of a tree just behind
the old bull's shoulder. I can see him chewing the cud in
the dappled light. The trigger is squeezed. The enormous
bullet, with its New Year's worth of gunpowder, crashes
like the final trump. Though I can't feel a thing, the sight
jerks up and for a moment I'm blind. I look back, and
where I thought there was only a pair of old buffalo there
must be 20. The bush splits and splinters all around us.
As they pound away, I crank the bolt, spilling bullets into
the leaf mould. And there, 50 yards away, my bull bellows
a furious, accusatory, pitiful and brave last post, staggers
and slips sideways, its lungs full of gore. It is an amazing
and terrible thing. It touches some atavistic drive. It is
a narrative and a feeling I can't compare to any other
civilised aesthetic ethicurean thing I've ever done.

The bull is skinned and jointed in 20 minutes. He's
thrown into the back of a Toyota truck, and that night we
eat oxtail soup and boiled tongue. The rest of his bulk
is hung in strips to be dried and taken home to villages.

We leave the circular miles of gaseous gut to the vultures that circle and fall like a centrifuge from a pulled plug.

There is in the hunt a tangible sense of being part of a rough and violent scheme of nature. That may be as spurious as the rush of a fairground ride, but nonetheless it's a moment of something. Something gripping. Something wordless. Something instinctive.

Dream world

Take a trip to Vienna and in no time at all you'll understand why Freud came up with psychoanalysis.

If you're one of those well-balanced people who think that psychoanalysis is only for sad folk who don't have enough friends to buy them a beer and to tell them to stop being such a big girl's sponge bag and take their thumb out of their mouths and bury their self-pity under a couple of good jokes about nuns and cucumbers or just to take a couple of doses of mindless exploitative sex by way of treatment, then you really could do with a long weekend in Vienna. Anyone who thinks Sigmund Freud needed his head examined and who knows a bloke who caught his father giving himself a Brazilian with wax from an altar candle while he happened to be wearing his sister's underwear and eating figs out of a stiletto and he's still a straight-up guy who's never had a trick-cyclist moment, then you really should think about spending some time in Vienna.

After two hours in the city you suddenly understand Freud and the whole analysis thing. It all makes sense. Or at least it makes perfect sense to the Viennese. They are quite possibly the most unexpressive and repressed people you'll ever meet en masse, and that includes Eskimos in January. Somewhere outside Vienna there is a mass grave where they've buried all their emotions.

Freud could have only come up with analysis in Vienna. This is dysfunction central. In fact, I've always wondered what would've happened to mental illness if Freud had lived in Brazil and Jung in Ghana. (It is a known tonto fact that all nutters go doolally sycophantically to please their doctors. So Freudian patients have Freudian fruit-loops, and Jungians are two Jungian sandwiches short of an ego picnic.) Brazilian analysis would've been quite different to Austrian. Vienna is the Greenwich Mean Time of bats in the barn. To start with, the city looks like a very elaborate, very disturbed dream. You walk through streets of buildings encrusted and barnacled with obsessive frotting decorations and it makes you wonder who planned them and whoever said, yes, that's exactly what we're looking for, with a lot of flying angels and eagles with crowns fighting the fish people over the front door. And I like the 20-foot naked elves holding up the stable.

Vienna is a plaster-and-marble porn show of violent nudity. They're everywhere; look up and there's always a straining buttock looking back at you. This all obviously started off as being a bit of neoclassical decorative fun and municipal showing-off but soon it became a vast art-therapy class of collective neuroses. Vienna is one big dream therapy session. You look at the pulsating, perky and penetrative porticos and then you look at the Viennese walking underneath them and you realise that they're thought bubbles of unconscious desire, the mumbling of the Austrian id. What you'd never guess by just looking at them – conservative, straight-laced and buttoned-up to the neck, hatted and polite and quite polished. And nutty as a chipmunk's breakfast.

The result of the surreal culmination of this righteous probity with the marble profligacy is to make everything seem like a Freudian slip. Waiters arrive and leer, 'Would you like cream on that?' and you feel yourself blushing, and every single waiter says it. 'Do you want cream on that?' About everything. Cream and whipped cream are the optional extras to all of Austrian gastronomy, and, one suspects, quite a lot of other Austrian life as well. Every culture has its endemic condiment: chilli, ketchup, mayonnaise, vinegar, mustard; Austrians like their cream. After a bit you realise there are few things that aren't improved by a fatty, frothy Freudian squirt.

I predict that Vienna is set to become this year's fashionable European city. We've had a couple of decades of discovering the great baroque and Baltic cities from divided Europe and now Riga and Prague, Budapest and Tallinn have been swamped by stag parties and boy racers rallying Porches across the autobahn of socialism for charity, and it's time to look again at the unfashionable Old World Europe, and you can't get much more unfashionable and Old World than Vienna. It doesn't even make an effort to get with it. Occasional excrescences of Euromunicipal public-space sculpture look even more absurdly temporary and graffiti-like in Vienna than they do in other places.

The conservative nature of the city is a lot of its charm. People here aren't friendly, they're polite, and once you get used to the idea that the waiter isn't going to ask you how you are and tell you his nickname and mention how great you're looking or compliment you on your choice of water, but just say good morning and ask what you'd like, it's actually a blessed relief. You walk through the opulent shopping streets and look at the goods crammed into them and you realise that this is a city from a time before life's long diet and guilty consumption. Before fur was a moral issue rather than one of insulation. Where it was decided that tradition will always trump innovation.

This may lead to a sort of entrenched, institutionalised collective conservatism, but after years and years of chasing the new and the latest thing, and after the ever-changing menu of experience and entertainment, it's nice to be relieved of the relentless urban chores of the contemporary. More than a relief, it feels somehow adult. Vienna is undoubtedly a grown-up city, and has been for a few hundred years. Their neuroses and dirty little obsessions come from before the First World War. Vienna may be mad, but it's old mad. It's been spared the whole 20th-century me-me-me New-Age fashion therapy and the self-absorption of the modern age. Here men and women aren't from Venus or Mars, they're from Innsbruck and a very good family in the Tyrol.

And it makes you realise how much of travel is an excuse to not behave your age, to slip the leash of responsibility and commitment. Abroad gives us permission to drink, behave, letch and, worst of all, dress like our teenage selves. It's about being childish, and Vienna isn't like that. Restaurants don't have a dress code – they don't need one because Vienna has a dress code. You dress your age, and appropriately to dine with other grown-ups. And only when you're wearing a jacket and tie can you get an infantile whipped-cream moustache.

Snail's pace

- -

***There is something undeniably
appealing in the idea of slowness
– as long as you don't actually
need to be anywhere.***

On November the 11th last year, I found myself in an
airport. They had the two-minute silence at the 11th hour.
We stood, most of us, beside our suitcases, heads bowed.
It was the most uncomfortable two minutes I've ever had in
an airport. Airports are designed and imbued with a sense
of lateness, of rushing. The whole ethos of an airport is the
hurry and scamper of infuriation and clock-watching. It is
dozens of time-zones pressed, one on top of the other, in
an unforgiving and relentless box.

The Slow Food movement begat the Slow City
movement. It is now something of a force for change
in Europe. It'll be a slow change. There is something
immensely attractive about slowness. Something that
becomes languorously. We think of those lunches that turn
into tea and then cocktails. Of flipping the sign on the
shop door and taking an hour on the couch. Everything
you think of with slowness comes with an accompaniment
of sybaritism. Slow soup, slow-ripened peaches, slow
kisses. Strolling and sauntering and occasionally lolling.
A handwritten note, a hand-picked posy of flowers. Setting
the table properly with the right knives and forks and
enough glasses and everyone sitting down to eat and chat.
Reading books with a hat on. (You, not the book.)

And then if you ever actually do get to spend some time, any time at all, in a slow city, you see what it's really like. Try Istanbul or Bombay or Rio or the thousand other fractious, jammed, infuriated, smoking, honking, frustrated places. Try driving through rural Madagascar for six hours in second gear because there's not a road that could accommodate third. If you want to know the dystopian side of slow, ask yourself, would you want a slower internet or a slower shower?

The Slow Food and Slow City movements are attractive in a pre-Einstein way. You'll remember the old German with the fast hair pointed out that time is relative, and what is relative for you is the time between pushing the button for the lift and then pushing it again because you imagine the lift has a shorter attention span than you do and may have forgotten that you're here waiting. The relativity of time of you ordering a beer and the waitress bringing it is also, for the waitress, the time between you ordering the beer and then asking her again if she's forgotten the beer when she's been on her feet for four hours, there are three other tables waiting for their bills and you look like the sort of bloke who thinks a tip is a place you put your rubbish. A quickie means quite different things to different people. A quick drink is never quick, nor is it ever singular.

The Slow Food and Slow City movements speak to a terrible yearning of urban folk, people who feel the timing of their lives has been taken out of their control, who are being forced to run faster and faster by the collective aspiration and fear of others. The relative time isn't the gap between their pushing the lift button and then pushing it again; it is the gap between their buttons being pushed and then pushed again. Cities push all our buttons like

Turkish taxi drivers push their horns. Ideally we would like to move at a leisurely pace through a town where everyone else is sprinting. Which is essentially what you do when you go on holiday: you meander around somebody else's day from hell.

There is an inescapable feeling that the collective button-pushing time is speeding up our lives. That we live more like fruit-flies than our fathers and that they lived shorter times than our great-grandfathers. The horse was replaced by the car, then the plane, then the internet, so the music of time has gone from a waltz to a jive, to a body-popping breakbeat. There is an uncomfortable feeling that every new invention that cuts time's corner to make time slip more sympathetically in fact forces us to run ever faster. The convenience is only ever an assistance to some previous machine, so that live music gives way to wind-up gramophones and then the wireless and CDs and iTunes. Each one benefits the technology, not the violinist, nor indeed the audience.

This is an old man's gripe, the feeling that I'm becoming Schrödinger's cat. You will all remember that Schrödinger's cat is trapped in a box with a particle of decaying atomic matter, and it may be both dead and alive simultaneously, and it'll only become one or the other when the box is opened. I don't understand it either. But I know that we often feel like cats in a box, both running and stationary, fixtures of a mad German-scientist thought-experiment. Schrödinger also invented a new word to go with his morbid-vital moggy: *verschränkung*. I think it means messed-up, confused and complicated. I don't know. But it sounds like the way I sometimes feel.

I travel because when you move at a different pace from your own environment you can be very speedy in slow towns and you can put your feet up in hectic ones. You dance to an internal beat that is not yet synchronised to the place you're in. One of the greatest pleasures is to eat fast food at your leisure. To queue up with the clock-watching locals as they shuffle for their slice of pizza, or click their fingers for their tortilla. To sip a second cup of coffee in the early morning commuter-rush to offices, eating other people's time. It's like picking the minutes out of their pockets.

And, cantankerously, I always keep my watch on the time of the place I've just come from. It denies the imperative of the local, remains aloof and above the herd. It doesn't need to speed. It's like Schrödinger's watch – one time caught in a locked canister in another time, both alive, both ticking away, together but separate.

Here in England, sales of oranges have plummeted. It's not that people don't like oranges – they drink gallons of orange juice – it's just that they can't find the time to peel one any more. Or rather, the thought of the time it would take to peel an orange seems excessive or extravagant. So they will forgo the pleasure of a well-peeled orange. I remember my grandfather used to peel one every Sunday after his nap. He carried a small silver knife for the purpose. It was as much craftsman's pride as anything. It was a prophetic Slow movement and he did it not so much for the orange, but because he'd been in the trenches, spent four years without fresh fruit. He took the time to peel it and give a perfect segment to his grandson as an act of atonement and remembrance for the blokes who never would.

Ancient isle

Where in the world could you literally be anywhere on earth? Mad, mad Madagascar of course.

'Where are we?' asked Tom the photographer. It's somewhere with an unpronounceable name. Obviously not unpronounceable for the inhabitants of wherever we are, just us visitors. 'No,' he said, 'what country are we in?' We arrived together. You had the tickets. There's a stamp in your passport. You know which country we're in. 'No,' he said again, forcibly, 'what I mean is, if you didn't know what country we were in, where would you think we were, and would you think that perhaps we might be where we are?' Right, let's have a look.

Where we precisely are is in a small restaurant eating meat and rice and chilli sauce. The room's cheap. It has votive pictures of Christ and his mum, and fairy lights. It's unmistakably Catholic. There are other people here. They look a bit Latin American, a touch southern Indian, a little bit northern African. There's a woman with an elaborate '50s hairdo and a man wearing a woman's Sunday church hat without irony or, as far as I can tell, insanity. There's another man in a suit with a pork-pie hat. Outside, the street looks sort of French, colonial, perhaps a bit West Indian. Run-down poor two-storey shophouses, but polite and nice. The road's more holes than road. And there are human rickshaws. There are very few places in the world that still have human rickshaws, and there's a big old

Asian cow with a hump being reluctantly dragged by the nose by a small boy who is definitely African. It's hot. And it's a conundrum.

We could be in Central America. Brazil, the Bahamas, the French bits of the Caribbean. Beyond the town, the landscape looks like central Asia in part, and Bali in another part. This is the most unexpected, mixed-up place I can remember. 'It's mad,' said Tom, 'really mad.' And indeed that's exactly where we were: Madagascar.

This place, or these places, confirms a theory I've been incubating about the shape of the world. Countries that've been surrounded by sea grow up different from everywhere else. Nations whose borders are random lines in the sand or the snow or run along rivers or roads may not like their neighbours, but they grow to be like them. It's a homogeneity that grows from propinquity, whether you like it or not. You only have to hang out in the Middle East for a couple of days to be surprised by how similar all the furiously denouncing and competing groups are, how similar their demands, how similar their fury, how it all seems like a series of echoes. European countries merge, one into the other, till at the edges they all become Monaco, or Switzerland or Holland or Belgium or Luxembourg. But the islands – the UK, Ireland, Corsica – are all still distinctively, for better or worse, their own places. It's a geographical version of the old human quandary: are we formed by nature or nurture? Are countries made by culture or geography? Islands prove, I think, that geography makes people what they are.

The most socially distinctive places I've ever visited are, in order, Cuba, Iceland, Haiti, Tasmania and Madagascar. Island people become vital and exotic. They make up stories about themselves and have obsessive fantasies and shared superstitions because over time those shared tics and eccentricities become communally held character traits. All people from small islands dance funny. When in Cuba, it's funny, but brilliant and original, spectacularly erotic and deeply enviable, but it's still odd. Cubans dance all the time. In the queue for the chemist, sitting down, in their sleep. Icelanders also dance weirdly, with strange Nordic exuberance, like men with imaginary salmon down their pants. As soon as we landed in Madagascar, I said to Tom, we've gotta find some dancers, they're going to be terpsichorean gold. And they were. A sort of synchronised flashing, with cramp, to music that is the African version of the Macarena, played on guitars made out of fruit boxes.

People haven't been in Madagascar all that long. Still new here – still learning the ropes. A mere 1300 years. The oldest island on earth with the youngest human inhabitants. Actually, Iceland's younger, by about 500 years. The original refugees here didn't come as you might expect from Africa just over the way, but from right across the Indian Ocean from Indonesia. Later, people did come from across the strait from Mozambique to make a singularly attractive half-Asian, half-African people who rise above the sum of their parts and, thanks to a brief spell of French colonialism and some English Methodist missionaries, are split between Catholicism and Protestantism, which is really only the wrapping that hides their old ghostly beliefs in extreme ancestor worship.

They've nurtured an extreme dysfunctional hybrid that transcends its heredity and its history. They have become the children of an astonishing geography with 10 distinct climates and habitats and more indigenous green things than anywhere else on earth. The Malagasy have gone about transforming their island, planting the rice they must've carried carefully in their outrigger canoes from Indonesia and herding the humpbacked cows that may have come from southern India or Africa. If you're a conservationist or a New-World earthful ecologist, then the arrival of humans in Madagascar has been an unmitigated disaster. They have for a thousand-odd years rigorously burnt away the forest, made extinct several species of lemur and the largest bird ever to stand on this land, the mythical roc.

But ecologists and environmentalists always think that about people. They never look at humans as anything other than the problem to be blamed and fettered and laden with collective historical guilt. They've never looked at our beauty and ingenuity and the vivacity of people and what they build and grow and the lives they spin. Malagasy are as fascinating and as memorable as any of the weird species on this island. The burnt landscape that was created for the cattle and the rice is just as astonishing and memorable as the forest. The unlikely combination of Asia and Africa in this land is miraculous and wholly unexpected.

Australia and Madagascar have a very particular thing in common. It's the baobab. There are said to be nine species of that remarkable hollow tree that the bushmen of the Kalahari say was planted upside-down by an angry devil. Seven of them exist only here in Madagascar. One lives in Africa and one in Australia. A keepsake, a souvenir from a time when all three were part of the über-daddy continent Gondwana.

Quickly, without looking, what's the capital of Madagascar? If you knew it was Antananarivo, buy yourself a beer. Now say it to the person sitting next to you. If you managed without stuttering, giggling, repeating, spitting and arriving at no fewer and no more than six syllables, buy everyone in the office a beer. It is the most impossible language. It sounds like Swahili spoken with an African accent and it loves syllables almost as much as it loves As. They insert extra As wherever they can. It's a language that could only arise on an island. It's not meant to be spoken by outsiders. John Donne made the oft-repeated clichéd observation that no man is an island. It's a truth about men, but it's also an implied truth about islands, that they stand apart. That they're not like other lumps of land. That the things that happen on them only happen on them. Visit Madagascar – while stocks last.

Galling the Gauls

France's allure may have faded for some but it will always be the model of worldly sophistication.

Every year I go to France, to the same place in Provence. I do the same things. I go to Saint-Rémy and drink café crème, pick at a croissant, and read two-day-old English papers, trying to ignore all the other Englishmen doing the same things around me. I buy another pair of rope-soled espadrilles that will grow sticky and uncomfortable and join the other 48 pairs in the basement cupboard. I buy lavender oil, though actually the finest lavender comes from the south of England. I go to the fromager and get three sorts of chèvre and wait for an age as the assistant wraps them as if they were a present for an ancient aunt. I go to a market in my new shoes that slip and chafe and I'll buy five sorts of olives and some figs and little packets of sausage and some pâté and a jar of confiture de fraise des bois and probably a new crew-necked, long-sleeved stripy T-shirt, unwearable unless you're going to a fancy dress party as Picasso. I will listen to passing accordionists, resist a beret, and watch women walk small dogs.

Oscar Wilde said that when good Americans die they go to Paris. Well, when liberal intellectual insecure Englishmen die they go to a queue for a cheese stall in a Provençal market. It is where everything we associate with *la bonne vie*, the *déjeuner* without end, exists, and I for one wilfully ignore the truth. That the cheese is made in Holland, the saucisson comes from Poland, that the shoes are from Croatia, the T-shirt was made in Bangladesh, the figs are from North Africa, as is the girl who sold them to me, and everyone else is probably Albanian or a Gypsy or an Englishman like me, pretending to be French. Everybody's pretending to be French.

Like other Englishmen, I manage to have selective partial vision. We only see what we need to see to maintain the fantasy of old France. But I must admit it's getting harder. France is becoming a virtual country, like an old computer game you play on the back of your eyelids. For 200 years France and the French have been the arbiter if not of culture then of the cultured life. It was always a bit of a fraud, a self-delusion, but it was based on some very solid, civilised foundations. Post-war France was the world centre for almost everything that made you feel sedately superior. Films, novels, art, fashion, design. And the food.

Now, one after the other, like insouciant dominoes, they've fallen. French films have withered into dire, horrible self-reverential bores or desperate, unfunny comedies. (A sense of humour was never a terribly French thing.) French books: do they still write French books about anything other than politics and gossip? French fashion doesn't exist. The French names are all run by Italian and English and German designers. Art, it must be admitted, was mostly done by foreigners living in Paris or the south of France, but that was fine because they wanted to live in Paris or the south of France, and the art seemed to come from the place that offered them licence and light, a certain *je ne sais quoi*. French art today has flatlined. French design is a pretentious joke. And worst of all, saddest, is French food.

In many ways it has remained the same, only in far fewer places. As in England, where there is a congenital disease which is killing off pubs, so across the channel it's the bistros which are withering. The prix-fixe menu of a few francs for a mound of rillettes and a steak frites or a plate of tripe, a small tranche of fish in beurre blanc, followed by some brie or poached prunes or tarte fine, all going, turned into pizza or kebabs. French food has remained, but everyone else has changed. Attitudes and diets have changed, and the chefs' attempts to mutate bourgeois cuisine, to lighten it and slim it, have made it ridiculous. The ingredients that French food comes from, that astonishing obsession with the finest things that could be grown or plucked or bottled, the most labour-intensive manufacture for the smallest possible production by a peasant society, are all dead. The infinitely fine filigree of artisanal markets is threadbare and cynically manipulated and bought up by brands hiding behind folksy labels.

What has France left in its cultural waistcoat pockets? Well, French philosophy is still as screamingly risible and portentous and irrelevant as it always was. And French pop songs remain the most awesomely naff and brilliantly crap musical moments ever conceived, every one of them some mayonnaise-voiced doggerel attempt to squeeze one more syllable into a line than it can comfortably or rhythmically accept. The French still think pop songs are essentially poems stuffed into tunes, and they still imagine that the words matter. And stoically and absurdly, like a man who always carries a condom and a red rose because he knows that one day the right girl is going to fall off her bicycle at his feet, the French wait for the Charles Trénet, Edith Piaf-zeitgeist thing to come around and bathe them

again in rightness. In the meantime there is French rap
to be avoided.

Being from the gauche side of the channel, I should
of course spend a moment in sniggering glee at the
precipitous decline in French culture. What is left is now
a rootless and meritless French arrogance, which simply
makes them funnier and more pathetic, like paunchy men
standing in Europe's drawing room, dressed only in their
Speedos. I should giggle, drain my cup of schadenfreude,
but really I can't.

France was always our idea of heaven. Paris was the
city I yearned to be transported to as an art student.
My lust still remains caught on the sulky, petite,
smokewreathed women of the New Wave. I will ever be
drawn to French art and French style. I hope to go out in a
surfeit of foie gras and cassoulet. It's my age. France has
always been the model of sophistication for men like me,
and I'm too old to find some new fantasy.

But not my children. They will only read Camus if they
have to sit him for some exam. They want to eat burgers
and curry. They think that Angelina Jolie is the sexiest
thing on celluloid. Fashion is an international scrum
of strange, exotic branding. Art is Brit and Jap. Their
cultural world doesn't even have a hole in it where France
used to be. France has the same cultural standing for
the young as Finland does. (Possibly less than Finland;
Finland has Nokia.)

France is now a museum for the old. It is a great open-
plan retirement home for the Englishmen who can't wear
shorts and are still meaning to read Proust under a peach
tree. The rather glorious truth about France's extinct
culture is that it died out for good Darwinian principles.
It had reached a point of almost perfect equilibrium,

and a change in the balance of suavity, manners and impetuosity, intellect and flirtation would've been to diminish the whole, so they waited for the world to regret its bad taste and come back to le vie Française. But they didn't, of course. Except us portly Englishmen, and a handful of aesthetically fine-tuned American gays, which is rather galling for the French. But they're right. Better to die an unmodified, unrepentant, ridiculous Frenchman than to live on as some Eurotrash ersatz mongrel.

Song sung blue

We've got an inane ditty for birthdays, so why not bless other noteworthy occasions with a similarly discordant sentiment?

I walked across a beach, and in 30 seconds, I knew it was the worst beach in Minorca. The sea was fine, the sand was okay, the view was lovely, it was clean and sheltered. I got off it as soon as I could. People occasionally ask, where are the best beaches in the world? And I always reply, it depends on who you're with. But I can tell you how to tell the worst beaches in the world: they're the ones with the bare-naked people on them. Not bare naked because they don't own clothes, though if you do find yourself on a beach with committed lifetime 24-hour naked chaps, it's probably in the Nicobar Islands and they're about to kill you with barbed spears. No, I mean people who live and work all wrapped up and who come to the beach specifically to get utterly and butterly naked. In short, Germans. Proto-spiritual Germans.

There is a seaside global truth that says the worst bodies wear the smallest trunks, and the very worst wear none at all. It's the aesthetic horror of people who think that being nude will show the rest of the world what beautiful people they are on the inside. Their nakedness is a billboard not for nubility or sensuality, but for rigorous ethical housekeeping and moral mountaineering. And if that were all, we could just laugh at them. But the fact is

------

that naturist beaches are the most bad-tempered radiantly sociophobic stretches on the planet. You know the dream where you find yourself naked in a public place and you wake up in a sweat and wonder what it would feel like if it happened for real? Well, all you have to do is walk down a nudist beach wearing clothes and feel the glares of scorn and the ugly muttering anger of naked intolerance. Nudist beaches are the only places I'm tempted to moon people.

I'm also often asked for insiders' tips on being able to tell a good restaurant from the other sort. My advice is to enter, ask for a menu, order some food, and when it arrives, eat it. Generally the inquirers are not satisfied with this. We could have thought of that, they say, implying that if that was all there is to being a restaurant critic, then I'm taking my pay cheque at best under false pretences and at worst under pretend pretences. What they want is a tip, a secret inside sign. Okay. Well, don't eat in a restaurant that has ankle-deep pools of vomit outside or a chef who's picking his nose or is being picketed by slaughterhouse workers.

Granted these are unlikely-to-rare sightings, but here are two things that never, ever happen in good restaurants. Never eat anywhere that sets fire to things on purpose in front of you. Not pancakes, not Italian digestive. And never return to an establishment where the waiters sing 'Happy Birthday'. Nothing is so indicative of desperate sycophancy than the barbershop quartet of service staff warbling over a terminally horrified woman just coming to terms with being 50, who now knows she's got to eat a vile ice-cream cake with blue candle wax on it and then walk through a room full of people all thinking, thank God I'm a Sagittarius, remind me not to come here in December.

I heard somewhere that 'Happy Birthday to You' is the most pirated artist work in history. We've all stolen it. It belongs to the estate of some American woman. We should be paying royalties. What I want to know, though, is what on earth made her write it in the first place? What possesses someone to sit down at a piano and go, I know: what we really, really need is a song to sing at people on their birthdays. Had she always felt there was a song-shaped hole in the anniversaries of her birth every year? Whoever said: this would have been just a perfect day – if only there was a song you could all sing at me, preferably all starting at different times and in different keys and then halting at the personalised bit, like horses preparing to refuse a fence, while some of you call me by my given name, some of you use a pet name, a couple of you call me mummy, and those three at the back just mumble uh-uh because you've come as someone else's date and don't know who I am at all. Why isn't there a song for that?

So, Mrs Whoever-it-was sat down and said, what sort of song should this anniversary song be? Perhaps lyrical and romantic. Or maybe a dance, samba or waltz. It could be histrionic and hopeful. The words could be full of poetry and fondness. It might be amusing. Perhaps the whole thing would be best as a sort of Tyrolean drinking song? No, she thought. No, let's make it a blessed nursery rhyme, with words so crapulously bland and functional that even five-year-olds who've only heard it three times before make up pithier versions. Yes, that's what birthdays need – a nursery rhyme that will follow you around during your hopeless, gauche teens, your mate-hungry 20s, your sophisticated middle-age, your wise old-age and sage-like dotage, every year treating you like a stupid toddler.

After the invention of a birthday song, the most inexplicable thing is that anyone sang it twice. Not anyone, but everyone. How did we all know? Were there hymn sheets? Did they have a practice run-through? Were they all humming the tune in the kitchen before coming out with the cake? Now I think about it, I can't ever remember a time before I knew the tune for 'Happy Birthday'. Maybe it's hard-wired into our cerebellums. Perhaps we learn it, like whale song, through the amniotic murk, along with the theme for *Neighbours*.

I resent 'Happy Birthday'. I mind its cheery imbecility. I mind its predictable repetitive ersatz jollity. I object to the implicit invitation to strangers to lean over and sing at me as if I'm remedial, and to remind me that my mortal coil is unravelling. Mostly I hate it for not doing what it says on the tin. Happy birthday to you, happy birthday to you, has never, in all the countless times it's been sung, brought an extra watt of happiness to anyone.

And anyway, if you're going to mark small milestones of a life's course with song, why stop at birthdays? We already mark Christmas and national events, sport and death and marriage with specific songs. Why not a coming-out-to-your-parents song? Why don't we have a song and a cake for sleeping with a new partner for the first time? The waiters could come out with cake and a candle, and sing, *Happy rumpy to you, happy pumpy to you, get your knickers off, easy Sheila, rumpy-pumpy for you*. That would give you a warm glow on a first date. And what about a song for exam results, or for getting fired, or moving house? So raise your glasses, and all together, *Happy ...*

Catwalk cool

- -

In Svalbard, the most northerly inhabited place on earth, function takes priority over fashion.

Short is the new sweet, bum the new breast, tea the new lunch, poor the new rich, vintage is the new new. It seems that contrarianism is the new conformity. The 'new black' is a catchphrase that espouses and exposes the relentless search for innovation and the circular sameness of fashion.

It has always been attributed to Diana Vreeland, the ridiculous and venerable editor of *Vogue*, who actually once said pink was India's navy blue, which is funny, observant and anthropologically worth a student's dissertation. It was some other fashionista, I think Gianfranco Ferré, who actually said grey was the new black, which is gnomically dim, but then the '80s were the gnomically dim decade and the new black encapsulated the common garden-gnomishness of it all. By the turn of the 21st century, calling anything the new black had exhausted its frail profundity and worn out its nickel-plated irony. And then along came Obama and suddenly black was the new black and it had jumped from fashion and style to politics and civil rights.

This wasn't what I meant to talk about. I wanted to write about fashion and the cold because (I may have mentioned this before) I strongly believe that cold is the new hot and fashion is a vanity of temperate climates.

You can draw the Tropics of Fashion on a map. The northern line starts about five miles above London and the southern just off the tip of Sicily. If you continue those two orbits latitudinally around the world, between the two points you've pretty much encapsulated the Tropics of Fashion. Of course, there are clothes and choices and fashionable people either side of that but this is where fashion gets indented and arbitrated. This is where the new blacks are posited. This is the zone where the weather allows you the greatest variation in clothes and you can dress with an airy disregard for the sky. Go further south or north and the climate becomes your stylist. There are stylish people above and below the meridian but they tend to wear things that have been made not by designers but by experience and necessity.

When I found out I was going to go to Svalbard, a huddle of islands overseen by Norway that are the most northerly inhabited place on earth, I knew I'd need some advice on what to wear and I wasn't going to get it in the fashion department, from some editor who'd tell me that alpaca was the new cashmere and Dolce were doing some really butch biker boots that look warm.

Svalbard is 78 degrees north; the pole is 90 degrees. After Svalbard, there are only a few hunters, some climatologists, and adventurous nutters pulling sledges. It's cold. Really, really murderously cold. It was too cold for the Eskimos to ever bother living here. It's a place that is made up only and solely of weather. Big, white, mad, bad, bullying weather. But the Norwegians have a saying; they say that white is the new black. They also say there's no such thing as bad weather, only the wrong clothes.

So I asked a Norwegian what I needed and he gave me a list that was longer than the one for my boarding school uniform. There was not a single thing on it that I already owned. All the stuff I thought might transfer from Scottish autumn walking holidays was damned as being suicidal.

It wasn't just the amount of kit; it was the size and the volume. It started to arrive in my office and colonised a corner and then spread across the room like a glacier of goose-down, merino-wool waffle, wickable, breathable, impenetrable waterproof gear. I regarded it with an unbeliever's scepticism. Nothing here was constructed remotely by aesthetics. Not a single stitch or button was added to make the wearer look svelte, or handsome, or taller or sexier or better proportioned. I come from a place that would rather be wet and chilblained than ugly but chilblains aren't the price for getting stuff wrong up in Svalbard. Still disbelieving, I dragged a vast, waterproof North Face bag big enough to smuggle a gravid sow in up to the roof of the world. I stepped off the plane at Longyearbyen in my London tweed and the climate grabbed me by the lapels like a furious drunk. The scale of the weather here bore no relation to anything I'd waded through before.

My local guide said that if I wore gloves with fingers, I'd lose the fingers. You wear mittens. You wear boots with huge detachable inner boots of insulation that look like they've fallen off the space shuttle. If your feet get cold, you lose toes. You wear two balaclavas. The wind catches your nose or your cheek, it'll cut them right off. I put on everything I'd brought with me, layer after layer. Everything you wear has an understudy: socks have other socks, pants have bigger pants, jerseys come in pairs, so do jackets and trousers. My gloves had mittens. This is not clothing for comfort. The Norwegians dress for life. Get it wrong and you could lose a finger or your sight or the whole mortal coil. What you have to do, in effect, is turn yourself into a self-regulating ecosystem. You become a purpose-built micro-climate. And as cold as it got, which was bloody cold, 30 degrees below with a 40-knot wind shoving down the temperature, so cold that our smart modern technology ran out of figures to measure it with, wherever I stuck my face out or took off a mitten, it burned like frozen venom, like all-over toothache.

And I became immensely interested in other people's kit – but not in a fashionista sense, not in a 'Where did you get that bag?' way, but in a nerdy, mechanical way like boys talk about carburettors and torque. I'd ask about wicking and wool and weight and whether your socks had been organically lanolin washed. There was a relief in all this jargon, this heavy-kit chat. It was nice to be released from the insecurity of style, of taste.

I noticed something at the airport in Spitsbergen. The Norwegians are a remarkable weather-blasted, capable and bonetough people. You never see a fat one. I expect they leave them out on the glacier. They wear their skins tight-drawn over their angular bones like battened down, faded tarpaulin. They are admirable, attractive people who speak profoundly but seldom. To open your mouth unnecessarily is to waste hot air. And I also noticed that at the airport they were the best-dressed people in the world. In a postmodern Bauhaus-Corbusian sense, where form follows function, everything was carefully chosen for its practical application: the uniform of compatibility and outdoor competence. I realised that what they had was anti-fashion, given that the essence of fashionable style is to put on an attitude or an aspiration, to project a character, essentially to be someone you're not. What the Norwegians dress as is themselves so they can continue

being themselves. This season's look is the same as last
season's look. It's very, very damned cool. Freezing cool.
I turned to Tom, my photographer, who occasionally works
for *Vogue*, and I told him blonde is the new black.

Luxe gone wild

Glamour and camping have come together. They call it glamping, and the latest travel extravagance is a tent with a flushing bog.

I went to lunch with a big travel company, a big, big international holiday firm. I don't normally waste a lunch on business. It's that horrible hybrid: work, wheedling, and pretending to be social and chummy. Anyway, the food's invariably corporate-ghastly, and there's a presentation of unreadable brochures and a pen that doesn't work and a luggage label that I really don't want. Anyway, this time I went because, you know, I'm feeling sort of sorry for the travel industry. They're having a really horrid time. It's the inexplicable but rather enjoyable truth about the travel business that it provides the nicest, most fun and exciting weeks of our lives, and is consequently the most consistently reviled, railed against, sued and detested business in the world. This particular company trawls the expensive end of the market and so has to deal with some of the most irrationally bad-tempered customers in the world.

Now I expect you've noticed that the tempers in airports are short in exact relation to the shortness of the queues they're standing in. Economy will have a snake of several hundred people patiently shuffling their regulation-size suitcases along, reading books, chatting, and giggling with holiday anticipation. Business class will have a queue of 20 irritated people hissing at children called Tamsin and Roland and trying to corral skittish herds of matched baggage. They are regular travellers and therefore hate travelling. In the queue for first class, where there is a vase of real flowers, and an attendant of cinematic beauty and unparalleled diplomacy, there will be one fat woman in a fur coat who is having a histrionic tantrum, swearing banishment and humiliation to all the staff in the airport and a slow death in particular to the baggage handler because she has lost her mink face mask and they don't have her brand of moisturiser in the bathroom. As anyone in hospitality will tell you, other people's happiness is a miserable career, and the more happy you strive to make them, the more miserable they'll make you.

So I went to lunch, and they gave us the good news, which was that the market was very fluid and contracting and that many companies were going to find things very difficult and would go for long holidays never to return, but for people who could move with the prevailing climate, adapt to the sudden change in commercial environment, then there were great advantages to be taken. There were vast opportunities for the plucking.

My accountant has been saying much the same sort of thing: there are fortunes to be made in recessions, he says. And a banker I know mentioned darkly that some of his mates have never been richer. If this is all true, why don't we have a depression every other month so we can all have a go at being carpet-bagging plutocrats? They all look at me with a bland pity when I say things like that.

After the steamed sea bass and something chocolate over coffee, the travel bods got into their presentation and pointed out the bullet points on the screen. They came on like the mantras shouted by rugby teams in their dressing room before they go out and get flattened by the All Blacks. Luxury, apparently, is over. Conspicuous consumption is inconspicuous again. Gold bath taps, restaurants run by swanky chefs, are all over. Jewellery on the beach, rose petals in the bath, bikini bottoms floating in the Jacuzzi: that's also utterly, utterly passé. Apparently the rich still left with money and time to enjoy it don't want to look like the past-it rich, the over-rich or the idle rich with nothing but hedonism and hair extensions on their minds.

They, and by implication the aspirational bits of you, want an adventure. You want to learn something. You want to come home with more than pictures of a sun-lounger and an abused lobster. You want to boast about something that isn't a tan-line, and who you saw at the next table. You want to come back with a traveller's tale, a saga, not a holiday drink-alogue. You want to get out into the corners of the world that room service won't reach. The future of travel, I was told, is going to be [drum-roll; keen young executive flicks the button on his remote; and the screen flashes up, ta-ra ... a tent. A tent. That's it, a tent. The future of top-of-the-range holidays is a tent. What's the mass-market version going to be − a refugee camp? Oh no, no, you see I'm not looking closely enough. The images flicker across the screen. This is no ordinary tent: this is a tent you can stand up in, with a bed you can lie down on, with sheets that you could glide across, with a carpet, with mirrors and windows and a mosquito net that looks like interior design. This tent is to other tents what Ava Gardner is to other gardeners.

What we are about to yearn for is Scouting for liberals. And there's a name for it. It's called glamping. (That's glamorous camping for those of you who are slow at word and concept combining.) Never before have camping and glamour come together. Indeed, they've never been in the same sentence before. Camping is almost by definition the absence of glamour. But here we are, in the bush, in some distant savannah, on a river bank. There is a crackling fire on which a clever native bakes brioche and ciabatta in an old tin trunk. The Chablis is chilling, a camp table is set with napkins and a storm lantern. The only glitzy thing here is the Milky Way, and in the distance some questing creature calls. And sat next to you is a guide who has a degree in biology, astronomy, geology and anthropology, and a chest you could tee golf balls off.

And tomorrow it will all be gone, as if it had never happened. You will leave nothing behind; the whole lot will be packed away into a discreet 10-tonne truck and whisked off to another virgin caravanserai. You have the enormous smug satisfaction of owning not only a singular experience but an unimpeachably organic and green one.

This is a fantasy of ruggedness, a nursery play version of the wild. It is Marie Antoinette's weekend picnic farm, which is fine by me: given the choice between Marie's and a real farm, I'm with the French queen every time. What I mind about this is that however risible and embarrassing and tasteless big, expensive honeymoon holidays are, they do exist in real places and employ real indigenous people, and pay for somebody's economy, putting real kids through school so that they can grow up and be businessmen and come and have holidays with us. This Peter Pan camping adventure slips through the beautiful bits of the world leaving not a trace and very little cash.

I asked the man who was selling glamping to me what the most important thing about this new moveable feast was. He thought for a moment, and smiled, and said: 'Dimmer switches. And proper lavatories.' So there you have it. The latest must-have extravagance, the chic one-upmanship, is a flushing bog in the outback. We live in momentous times.

Cashmere if you can

Italians may lack a sense of humour, but Rome is still the ultimate holiday destination.

Someone once said that to be born Italian and male was to have won first prize in the lottery of life. I think it was me. I seem to remember that I added a caveat to the encomium – that to be born Italian and a woman was to have pulled a position between a fish and a dog from life's tombola. Italian men have gilded existences in direct proportion to their women's sullied ones. One of the reasons women have such a dowdy time in Italy is because Italian men are so much better at being women than they are. There is, beyond the Alps, that magical formula for being a properly masculine big girl.

Italian men shop better than most women. They care more about their appearance, their hair, their nails and the thread-count of sheets. Italian men have an unnatural affinity with cashmere. They're the only subspecies of bipedal hominid who can wear a pale pink v-neck sweater draped over their shoulders and go out in public, without it being part of some cruel dare or bet. They have apparently cracked the great mating conundrum, the design fault of mankind: how on earth do you have all the fun of being a bloke, with all the emotional range of being a bird? Italian men are able to talk on mobile phones for up to an hour. Not only is that way longer than any other style of man on the planet, it's longer than penguins can hold their breath underwater. Not only that, but they can do it while talking to other men.

I once wrote an article pointing out that the reason Northern European women loved Italian men was because it was like having a girlfriend with a willy. Which, incidentally, is why Italian women get such a hard time from them. It was a light-hearted, affectionate article, but it was noticed by the Italian press, who paraphrased it with infuriated exclamation marks, and a TV chat show called me and said they would fly me to Rome for the weekend and pay me a few hundred million lire if they could interview me. Fine. So I went.

The Maurizio Costanzo Show is a bit of an Italian institution and it's recorded in front of a large audience in a theatre. So, Maurizio asked, what did I mean by impugning the masculinity of Italian men? I smiled – a winningly Stilton grin, because obviously this was light-hearted joshing – and told him that, as we spoke, the European soccer cup was being played in England, and that the only national team that had made an official complaint were the Italians, who had wailed that there weren't hair dryers in their dressing rooms. I looked at the audience and waited for the chuckles of recognition and the guffaws of self-deprecation. Silence. And 2000 people stared back at me with a collective 'and your point is?' expression.

Naturally the Italian men would complain that there were no hair dryers. Look at their hair. They had beautiful hair. It was a national treasure. And it was typical that the English, a cold philistine nation that fried fish in pastry and cut their hair with breadknives because the bread was already sliced, were too uncivilised to put hair dryers in dressing rooms. And what about the foot spas and

manicure sets? It was at this moment, wallowing in the
hostile Latin embrace, that I realised another great truth
about Italians of all genders. They have absolutely no
sense of humour.

After the show, we went and had dinner and I walked
through the city. It was summer, and it was warm and
clear. I'd never really been to Rome before. I'd been to
Italy dozens of times, flown into Rome and driven out.
I'd been saving the Eternal City for a special occasion.
We walked through a series of opera sets. One square
led into another like scene changes. We went to a party
in a palazzo that had been built by Michelangelo. They
all spoke Italian and wore cashmere sweaters over their
shoulders, so I stared out the window at the frieze of
black cypresses, cupolas, domes and columns silhouetted
against the navy blue sky, and I smelled the evening
pines, wine and the dust of ages, and listened to the
mopeds and the tinny hee-haw of Fiat police cars and the
incessant babble of Italians talking on mobile phones.

I knew in that moment two things: one, that the reason
Italians don't have a sense of humour is because they
don't need one. The point of jokes and having a laugh is to
cheer yourself up, to make a miserable life a little better.
If you live in Wigan, you need a sense of humour. Italian
men don't need to swap jokes because they are already
quite happy being Italian men. What Italians have instead
of jokes is a boundless, inexhaustible sense of fun. All
the things that made you chuckle before you could walk
continue to make an Italian laugh until he dies. Italians
love to tickle each other. You'll see middle-aged men
in business suits tickling each other in the street and
squirming happily. They also pinch, slap, ruffle, chuck
and talk in falsetto voices. It makes them happy.

The second thing I realised was that, from now on, every year that I didn't spend some time in Rome would be wasted, and if I were allowed only one more trip to one more place in my life, it would be here, without a second thought. All the other options – the magic places, beaches, cities, mountains, deserts, rivers, cottages, palaces and sandcastles – faded in comparison to Rome. It isn't just the beauty and the grandeur; it's the depth, the great experience of it. Rome knows more than any other place on earth. The word 'civilisation' shares a latin root with 'civic' – meaning city. This is the city that invented, grew and exported Western civilisation. And 2500 years later, it's still effortlessly the best at it. And thank God (who also lives here) it's looked after by the Italians. Imagine if Rome were a German city, or Hungarian, French, or Austrian? It nearly happened.

The next morning, standing in the Piazza Navona with a Roman friend, I asked dreamily: Why doesn't everyone live here? A millennium ago, the whole Western world dreamed of living in Rome. We could do it now. Why don't we all move here? Why don't we all have our offices in Rome?

Ah, he said, arranging his powder-pink cashmere sweater and regarding his reflection in a shop window, we thought of this. It is impossible. For starters, you need a miracle to get a phone connected here. To get a fax, you need to be the Pope, and even God can't get broadband. Nobody could do business in Rome. Scuzi ... and he answered his mobile.

Shore thing

- -

Most travel writers can't stand them, but beaches provide the most soulful experience you can find this side of the grave.

One of the very few things that all travel writers hold in common is an effete disdain of beaches. We don't do seaside, unless it's ironic or nostalgic. Beaches are for holidays, and travel writers don't do holidays. Holidays are for amateurs, pedestrians. A beach is a sandpit for grown-ups. It's an infantilising experience where the crowds regress through a childish, supine idiocy. On sand a man will wear toddler clothes in colours and patterns that he wouldn't dream of sporting on tarmac or carpet. You eat and drink stuff that would be disgusting under a roof. You play semi-skilled games, paddle geriatrically and get sunburnt. You stare toothlessly at bosoms and horizons. And all beaches are extensions of the same beach; they have a repetitive primary simplicity. We want them to do the same thing, which is essentially to regress us back to the holidays we remember with the romance of greening home movies.

Beaches dictate a certain sort of personality, a particular world view. It is, for instance, impossible to be sophisticated on a beach. And as I am prone to fits of meritless sophistication, I'm drawn to the antidote of beaches. Despite the travel writing, I do rather love them.

My childhood memories of them are invigorating
but not particularly more-ish. North Berwick, outside
Edinburgh, splashing in the North Sea: it was so cold
it was like being punched in the kidneys. I'd lose all
sensation below the waist. And I can still see the huddles
of spindly post-war children with concave chests and
sagging woollen trunks draped in balding cotton towels
looking like forlorn schools of forgotten penguins, teeth
chattering, eyes bright with hypothermia. Happy days. In
Britain, beaches are more endurance than entertainment.
I still have the niggling sense that there is something
wasteful about a hot beach. It seems a profligate waste of
the sun, being squandered just on sand.

I've just come back from Mozambique. I'd never been
before. It's not on many people's country wish-list, this
huge country sprawled on the east coast of Africa. It was a
collection of Swahili–Arab trading posts, slave ports and
smuggling, and then a Portuguese colony that continued
to trade slaves long after it was illegal, and smuggle ivory
and gold. The Portuguese were very bad at giving their
nicked bits of the globe back. They had to be terrorised
out of Mozambique and there was none of the polite
handover ceremony, the promises to keep in touch and
exchange students, which may be why Mozambique joined
the Commonwealth – just to spite Lisbon. Or perhaps they
fancied the Commonwealth Games and a Christmas card
from the Queen. (I've never really seen the point of the
Commonwealth; it's like having to have dinner with your
ex-wives.) Mozambique is a bit confused. It's doing its
best, but it has issues, resentments. It's the only country
I can think of that has a Kalashnikov on its flag.

In the north of the country, up by the Tanzanian
border, there is a long archipelago of coral islands. One

of these is Vamizi, and it has a resort with what they call oxymoronically in the travel business 'barefoot luxury'. That means handmade huts on a beach, comfortable and charming, but without a telly or a telephone, without WiFi or room service, just the sand and the sea and the weaver birds in the rafters.

The African coast of the Indian Ocean must be one of the least utilised tourist possibilities on the planet. There are barely a handful of African beach resorts. The coast is of a miraculously enchanting beauty. The sea is pale and warm; the diving, they say, is world-class; the sport fishing is spectacular. Nicola, my partner, caught a near-record giant trevally, and she's still beaming. It's supplanted our twins as her screen-saver. But what I particularly love is a beach with shells. I don't quite know why the combing meander of picking up shells should be so blissfully satisfying, or why its attraction and joy never seems to pall. There is something about shells that is so very precious and yet plainly free, so beautifully crafted, yet ubiquitous. And every morning, more of them are dumped on the strand, a tide line of miraculous carving, impossible intricacy; sea jewellery that comes with its own echo of the waves still inside it. This is the imitation of the shopping along with the antidote to consuming. They are infinitely precious and virtually valueless. They are pleasing to hold and Zenishly fascinating to peruse.

The reason I like beaches, and the reason travel writers don't, is that they have no narrative. They don't tell stories. They are atonal song cycles, mood without plot. And if you spend your life dissecting and reconstructing things into sentences and paragraphs, beginnings, middles and endings, then a beach, with its sighs and hisses, its slow breath, is a wonderful poultice. It makes no inquiries, demands no reactions. It fills your head with space and sounds and feelings. The sensations of an empty hot beach are as soulful as you can find this side of a grave. There is no end to this peace, just as Blake said, to see the world in a grain of sand, to pick up shells and see an infinity in your hand.

Nothing to do

It's about more than just time off; we think of ourselves as being at our most pure and best on holidays, and we strive for them to be of a different calibre to real life.

I just had lunch with a man who said he hated holidays. They fill him with dread. It's one of those things you really have to love. You can't say: I don't want my holiday, could I go back to work instead? It's somehow offensive, like saying you don't like sex or breakfast in bed. Actually, it's more acceptable to have gone off sex and eating breakfast in a prone position than to not take your holidays. Holidays are one of the few universal indefatigable human traits. Opposable thumbs, tears and looking forward to a fortnight away are what make us human. So when you say you don't like holidays, people ask to move their desks, don't let their children come over on play-dates and start divorce proceedings.

When did you first start having this irrational and antisocial loathing of recreational downtime, I asked. Right from the start, he said. I hated the first holiday I ever went on. The family took us away for a weekend at the seaside when I was seven. I was really looking forward to it. My mum told me how wonderful it would be and how much I'd love it, and what a good time we'd all have, and that there'd be ice-cream and fairy floss and sandcastles and donkeys and Punch and Judy and a pier and fish and chips. So what happened – it rained? No, the weather was fine, there was the ice-cream, fairy floss, sandcastles, donkeys, Punch and Judy, the pier, and there was fish and chips. They were dreadful. Horrible. It was such a disappointment. Why? Well, fairy floss is a filthy pink unpleasant cocoon, cheap ice-cream is like white pig fat (in fact, it is bleached pig fat), sandcastles are a silly bore, donkeys smell and have huge yellow teeth, Punch and Judy are sociopathic and if piers were streets on land you'd never go near them. I quite liked the fish and chips.

I see. So you were born a cynic, even at the age of seven. No, I was just born a realist. I've tried to go on holiday many, many times. Over the years I've been on at least 40 holidays and the best I've experienced is disappointment. Where was that? A weekend in Venice. That was very disappointing. But not as terribly disappointing as Istanbul. It is, he said, the expectation that sinks the holiday.

As well as being a realist, I am also an optimist, which combines to make me a fatalist. Whoever said it's better to travel hopefully than to arrive never went on holiday.

I have a feeling that quite a lot of people find holidays a bit of a strain, although of course they couldn't possibly admit it. The planning, the expense, the competitive photography. The obligation to have an experience that is of a different calibre to real life. Two weeks every summer that are a window into a higher existence. The holiday is your reward for work. More than that, our holidays are the definition of who we really might be if somehow we stepped up and had a more angelic existence. We like to think of ourselves as being at our most pure and best on holidays. This is all a modern construct. The very idea of a holiday is barely a century old in the sense of secular time spent doing nothing but indulging and pandering to pleasure. A holy day was conceived, as the name suggests, to be exactly the opposite – a religious moment of mortification, fasting and righteous self-analysis and purging. Work was what made you who you are. Toil was physically, intellectually and spiritually the purpose and obligation of existence. Not to work was mildly sinful. Travel outside business wasn't a pleasure; it was either an education or a cure. Restorative relaxing was what you had a garden and a rocking chair for.

I do have a great sympathy for all this. I rarely go on holiday; though I travel constantly, it's almost always work. And while it's almost invariably exciting, interesting and entertaining, it's rarely relaxing. And it's always fully engaging. But just a couple of weeks ago, the person whom I share a home and a family with said, that's it. That's it. Utterly, utterly it. I need a holiday and I need it now, and I need you to come with me. Well, of course. I've arranged, she said, for us to go to the Hotel Splendido in Portofino, on the Italian Riviera. We will do nothing. We will do nothing in elegant poses. We will do nothing covered in oil. And silk. And linen. We will do nothing in scented pools. We will do nothing under the stars, nothing under the sun.

I like a hotel that doesn't hedge its self-regard. If you call yourself the Splendido, then you'd jolly well better be splendido. And it is. It's indubitably the most splendido hotel I've been in. It was small without being bijou, smart without being chic, comfortable without being suffocating, and expensive without ... well, without embarrassment. The food is perfect: Ligurian. It's served as if service were a calling. Things that should be hot came hot and things that should be chilled came cold. Peaches were ripe, coffee intense and the pesto the best in Italy. And the other guests were so like the collected suspects from an Agatha Christie novel that you really didn't need to take a book to the pool, which was saltwater and hangs over a view that was everything your grandmother wanted Italy to be like.

A series of stepped gardens down to the tiny port where there are a couple of decent restaurants where you can eat baby squid and drink absurd cocktails made out of mutilated strawberries and watch the passeggiata. And reflect that, as holidays go, the Italians probably produce the best in the world. They invented the idea and have worked very, very hard indeed at apparently not working at all.

After four days, we went home. She was restored, refreshed and relaxed, and I must admit that I was perplexed. I had done nothing under the sun and it didn't bother me one bit. Which rather bothered me. So I wrote this, which made it work. And now I can relax.

The middle distance

----

*Middle America may be
universally canned, but there is
still something charming about
the land of the free and the people
who inhabit it. Oh, and the
blueberry pie is pretty good too.*

Cortez is a town in the south-west of Colorado. It sprawls
in an unconcerned just-got-up kind of manner between
the Navajo and Ute Indian reservations and the high Pine
Mountains and the aspen-fringed meadows of the San
Juan. Colorado is a square box that contains some of the
most good golly gosh astonishing scenery in the world.
If you think of Europe as being classically nature, Asia
impressionist, Africa expressionist, Australia naïve, then
America is nature's great big romantic period. America is
all strings and trumpet. It has the soaring emotion of high
romance and also moments of visual diabetes – just too
much syrupy brilliance.

   All students of international politics should come and
see the great American interior. Most of us are people
who made their countries, but Americans are people who
are made by their country. If you go out west you begin to
understand what makes Americans the way they are. I've
always had an unfashionable and unironic respect and
fondness for what is universally and dismissively known as
Middle America. It contains a lot of immensely admirable

people. Self-reliant, optimistic, determined, stoical, hard-working, rigorously honest, in fact, rigorously everything. And most of all, they're the kindest, most helpful folk I've ever come across. They are, it must also be said, prone to depression, possess a dull single-mindedness and a willful uninquisitiveness about anything they can't touch, smell, eat or tinker with. They're people whose horizons are broad but fixed, whose questions are few and answers simple. I like them. Clemenceau, the French politician, famously said that America went from barbarism to degeneration without an interval of civilisation. I bet he said it all the time. It has that smooth feel of a fond Gallic rudery. I bet he got a knowing laugh in all the Old World salons after dinner with that one. As with most glib French things – it's just plain wrong.

American civilisation is the cocktail of barbarism and decadence. This has been the look, sound and feel of our culture for the past 100 years. What is more true about America is that it went from austere hardship to immense comfort without an intervening thought for good taste. Comfort and ease, softness, smoothness, warmth, wrinkle-free, cosy, huggable things are what Americans like to surround themselves with. Relaxed is the aesthetic choice. The idea that you should suffer some inconvenience or mild discomfort for the sake of a look or an effect is an incomprehensible anathema. In this wide open space the elasticated lifestyle is all.

Towns like Cortez always look temporary, as if they're still auditioning for a place in the landscape. One morning you might drive past and find it's all gone, been blown away or swallowed up in the night, and it wouldn't be that surprising. All over Colorado there are remnants of communities that didn't quite make it, the ghost towns of

defunct businesses and mines. The Pueblo Indian remains
perched high up in the cliffs from tribes that were extinct
even before the Navajo and the Apache got here. For the
most powerful nation on earth there is a distinct sense
of impermanence about life on the land, as if it were all
on probation. And coming from the Old World where the
market towns and villages, the churches, manors and
castles all seem as immutable and resolute as the hills
and rivers, I find this exciting and refreshing. Because
if a mining or cattle town can spring up and die in the
architectural blink of an eye then, also overnight, the
prairie can sprout a Kansas or Chicago, the desert can
suddenly grow Las Vegas.

All over the US west there are communities made up
entirely of trailer caravans set in neat rows on tree-shaded
culs-de-sac plugged into the umbilical comfort of utility,
but they look like pieces on a Monopoly board, waiting
to be moved on, swept up by the story of the nation.
These trailers, so easily dismissed as white trash, as the
burrows of enigma and underclass, can also be seen as
the descendants of the covered wagon that first came and
prised open this vast nation, adding states a piece at a
time. America was only finished as a geographical entity
in my lifetime. It's been like some kind of gigantic jigsaw
puzzle waiting to fall into place. The drama of America
can never compete with its own set. It is dwarfed by the
land, the jagged height of the mountain, the heat of the
desert, the ferocity of the thunder. Why try to build a
house as beautiful as the prairie or as permanent as a
canyon? There's no beauty that can compare with the
beauty of nature. You can see how easy it is for this land
to become a fundamental cathedral, a huge amphitheatre
parable of the might of an elemental heaven and the

minute insignificance of individual humans. I think this is
one of the reasons that Middle America has such an oddly
resistant view of global warming and environmental crisis;
it's because it's so difficult to see it making a difference
on this scale. The forces of nature are so unarguable
compared to all human vanity and hubris.

And the nation itself was built on overcoming nature.
Americans don't live in their country, they live despite
it or perhaps with its benign disregard. The west is full
of tourists trundling around in caravans imitating wagon
trains, again, settling down in defensive circles in lay-
bys and almost all of them are American. They never
cease to be awestruck tourists in their own country. It's a
much-bandied truism that only less than 20 per cent of
Americans have passports. The assumption from outside
is that this is because they're frightened or ignorant
or too lazy to care how the rest of us live. But that's
not the truth. Well, it's not all the truth. They're still
getting to know their own backyard. In three generations
America has quadrupled in size. It's still fresh from the
oven. I travelled through a little town with one street of
clapboard houses, a café, a liquor store, a petrol station,
a few trailers. We stopped to eat cheeseburgers, they
recommended the blueberry pie. This is where they once
mined plutonium for the nuclear deterrent. This tiny blink
of a place was the well for the Cold War, the arms race, the
great game of global politics for 50 years. Now the holes
in the rock are filled in, the spoil bulldozed over, the river
runs muddy, boiling yellow alongside the road, the red
earth canyons blister in the sun. It's as if it all meant less
than nothing. The pie was surprisingly good.

Empty vessels

Once the epitome of moneyed gaucheness, the super-yacht is now a law unto itself, taking luxury to absurd new heights.

There are many bizarre sensations available to the connoisseur of contextual and tactile oddity. Flinging yourself down a spiral staircase bandaged in bubble-wrap. Running through wet sand in cashmere socks. Eviscerating a chicken blindfolded, using just your feet (only attempt this with a previously dead chicken). I'm having a sensation experience as we speak. I'm writing this in a bath at sea. Well, I'm composing this in a bath at sea. Actually I'm writing this on a plane 3000 feet above Turin. (You, I picture reading this lying in bed eating biscuits.)

The contextual tactile conundrum that always strikes me as odd is the bath-at-sea bit. It's watching the waves out of the porthole whilst inside I make ripples. The two expanses of water, separated by one thin hull: one warm, one cold; one salt, one soap. The sea is elemental, a metaphor for all emotion, sensuality and power and women. The bath is benign, thoughtless, bubbly and a bit of a soak. No one else I've ever mentioned this to finds the bath-at-sea contradiction weird or noteworthy.

In fact, they think I'm a bit weird for mentioning it at all, or for even noticing. The truth is I find almost everything about boats weird. I've never felt at home with boats, even though I come from an island and seawater is supposed to flow in our veins. I feel as homely on a boat as a haddock does in a cinema. But boats have grown to become a larger and larger part of travel. Ocean-going, opulently appointed boats are the divide between the them, which for the moment includes me, and the you, which includes you.

Forty years ago, pleasure boats were sporty and adventurous and a touch nerdy. They were owned by ex-naval men, men who wore nautical work clothes and were paint speckled and mildly whiffy. Boats were the aquatic version of caravans. Occasional Greeks had large pleasure ones dismissed as gin palaces, but altogether, boats were for fun, the damp equivalent of camping. Now boats are country houses, they're mansions, they're four-star hotels.

A contemporary of mine pointed out that when he was a lad he bought sweaty soft-porn mags. When he got his first job, he swapped them for car mags, and when he got to be more successful, aviation magazines. Now that he runs an international company he devours super-yacht periodicals. We always lust after the thing we just can't afford, and now super-yachts are the pinnacle of consumer aspiration.

The biggest private pleasure boat 10 years ago wouldn't be in the top 200 today. The Russian conspicuous-consumption fleet is almost as large as the military one. And the new super-yachts built for Californian internet cash and Russian utility bribes are so big that many of them can't get into holiday ports.

Boats have gone from being the means of exploring places to the places in their own right. They're not for holidays, they're floating memorials to your acumen. And what you sail to see is not interesting little islands or remarkable reefs or unspoilt, inaccessible beaches – what you go to see are other boats. The point of having that much money-haemorrhaging aspiration under your feet is to show it off to other billionaires who have opened up the money vein.

Super-boats have helicopters and their own motorcars, and now they're coming with submarines. I've been on one that had its own boardroom and office suite. Why would you want to have a perfectly drab, perfectly functional office with whiteboard and overhead-projectors on your dream yacht? Well, if you were part of the geeky pizza-and-brainstorms-in-the-shed internet plutocracy, then work was fun. In fact, work was probably the only fun you ever had.

The decorating of yachts is a small mystery. Why do they all have pictures of other boats in them, and then photographs of boats from the outside? And bars. A bar at home is the first word in grating naff hideousity. But on a boat, it's desperately chic, and Onassis had barstools covered in whale foreskins. That really impressed Jackie. On land she'd have made a face like a salted lime and remembered she'd left the gas on.

And then there's the staff. Obviously all billionaires have staff. You couldn't be a billionaire and do your own hoovering. But what is it about ozone that makes relatively rational landlubber plutocrats who are happy to hang out with yes-men in regular suits on land feel the need for a squad of gay sauna attendants and the cast of *The Pirates of Penzance* at sea?

You eat things on boats you'd never do on land, play games and wear clothes you'd never usually wear. Little things with shells and fish and nautical motifs, and men wear hello-sailor hats which they wouldn't put on for a bet on the pavement. Seawater does odd things when added to money. Boat owners outdo each other in all the childishly excessive ways that the rich have for outdoing each other. Better-looking staff, fancier cooks, more toys; bigger, faster, rarer. Last week I spoke to a breathless awestruck interior designer who'd been employed to do just the soft furnishings on a super-yacht. They were insisting on 1000 thread-count cotton sheets. If that means nothing to you, let me tell you it makes crêpe de chine feel like George Michael's chin, and one bed's worth will cost more than you spent on decorating your whole house. Of course, this isn't the point. If you've got a couple of billion, then the difference between goose and duck down doesn't really register. You could see boats as being a symptom and a palliative of an uncomfortable neurosis, of course. You could see it like that if it makes you feel better.

Boats are not about seeing the world anymore, not about adventure or being sporty and wearing an oily jersey. They're about control. The one thing all the rich men I've ever met have had in common was a pathological desire to organise the chaos of the world. A boat is a complete world on its own; you can micro-manage everything. A plutocrat can be Gulliver on his own Lilliput. In fact, if I ever get a yacht, I'm going to call it *Lilliput*. (By the way, boats' names are the novels that the super-rich and unimaginative have inside them.)

The one thing no one can command is the weather. Unless you have a boat. And then if the sun won't come to Ivan, Ivan can go to the sun. A yacht doesn't actually have to go anywhere, because it has already arrived.

Peak condition

- -

If you need to reconnect with something wild, head to the Scottish Highlands, where the landscape has no concern for your golf handicap, your bank balance or how many friends you have on Facebook.

There is one fixed point in my year. Actually there are dozens of fixed points: Christmas, birthdays, Easter, school terms, anniversaries, the office party, deadlines. My whole life turns out to be fixed points and deadlines, a slalom of imperatives. What I mean is there is one week that isn't fixed by other people, or the kids, or bosses, or God. What I mean is there is one week without noise. It's more a hole in the year, a blank in the diary, unsullied by asterisks and exclamations, scribbled phone numbers and restaurant names, an escape hatch in the space-time continuum. It's the week I spend in the Highlands of Scotland where I stagger and slip up and down the hills, gasping like a spilt carp, cold, wet, grazed, twisted, strained, agued and palsied. Every day of it, there is a moment where I swear, swear on my shuddering aorta, my turned ankle and my barbied lungs, that I will never, ever do this again. And then the minute I leave, I am yearning to get back, to dig this hole into next year's diary.

The purpose of being here is ostensibly to kill things. We go out accoutred for murder in camouflage with binoculars and guns and knives and sandwiches. But the pursuit of death is really only a ruse, a cover. As often as not the deer elude us. The point is really not death but the pursuit of life by life. To get out and discover quite how alive I still am. And the hills grow taller and my feet heavier, but still I'm bound to the wild pursuit in this quite literally breathtaking place. It is a validation that I still have a place in the landscape.

In this rough world there is a pleasure that is difficult to explain. This isn't about aesthetics or health or achievement or any of the urban unwinding, de-stressing, getting your head together stuff. It's something more basic, colder and ancient. It's being part of it, part of something bigger. The belonging not to a list of accrued things – the urban civilised litany of stuff that our credit companies and our censuses know about us – but to a species, to be Darwinian. To fit into a world that isn't already man-ordained or man-ordered.

There is a growing trend, particularly among middle-aged blokes, to choose holidays for their primordial discomfort. I'm noticing that a lot of chaps are packing rucksacks and heading out into the high country – up a river, over tundra. I know that holiday companies have noticed this too. There's a new market of sedentary men with families and white-collar jobs who don't want to exchange the vanilla comfort and safety of their homes for the fuchsia comfort and safety of some packaged and predictable resort. One tour operator who makes bespoke adventures for groups of men told me, 'These are people who want to come back with a story, not a tan.' Who want to have memories more than they want to have a set of

photographs just like the photographs they had last year
and the year before. How boring are most holiday snaps,
how passive.

Women tend to dismiss this as a midlife crisis thing
– possibly preferable to a Harley, a ponytail and a mail-
order mistress, but still essentially risible, a foolish-man
fantasy game, an attempt to ignore the truth and put off
the responsibilities of life. But in fairness that's not it.
'Midlife crisis' is such a dismissive, glib little put-down.
It's more complicated and more poignant than that, than
just wanting to feel 18 again.

Most of us reach a point where we've already hacked
the big stuff. We've had kids and wives, we've had careers
or had them thrust upon us, we've taken on mortgages
and debt. And we've handled it. We've been okay at the
grown-up stuff. We really don't want to be teenagers
again, or wear leather, or go to nightclubs. We know what's
ridiculous. And if we're not actually proud of our lives,
then we're pleased with them; what we've made, the things
we've achieved. But there is also a nagging sense that
we've become janitors in our own lives. We turn up and
maintain stuff – paint a wall, unblock a drain, shout at the
kids, put out the rubbish – and with care and luck we can
go on doing this forever.

But we didn't set out to be curators to our own families
and offices. There is a disconnect with something wild,
something out there. So we get on a horse, or into a canoe,
or onto skis; we pack a sleeping bag, a wet-suit, goggles
and a mosquito net and take a week to face the weather.
It's not escapism, or fantasy, or role play, or showing off;
it's being a bloke who hasn't hyphenated himself with
father, or husband, or neighbour, investor, accountant,
teacher, plumber, journalist. Because out here in the

Highlands, with the heather and the gorse, the ravens and the stags, they don't care. The landscape has no concern for your golf handicap, your bank balance, how many friends you have on Facebook.

I'm from Scotland and this is also a week of homecoming. Like most of us I have contradictory feelings about all that root stuff, but I do have an emotional commitment to this place that has grown fond through absence. I only went 500 miles away down the road, but still this is the Other Country, and I suspect the adventures men take on are often bound up in the business of their childhoods. We think it's serendipity or an empirical choice, but to walk or cycle or run in deserts, or hack through jungle will have had its origin in a bedtime book, a moment with your dad, the first time you realised the world went on beyond the bottom of the garden. It belongs to a bit of your brain and memory that is not rational or explainable. This week in the hills chasing the deer isn't really a hole in the diary; it's not an escape. It's the ridge pole of the rest of the year. It takes a load for all of the other stuff.

I don't want to live up there. I have no intention of chucking the solid bit of my life away. I come back to it with greater gusto and gratitude knowing that I'm not just the sum of my achievements, my habits and my acquisitions. When I'm stuck in traffic or a tedious meeting, when the computer crashes and the deadlines pile up, I can close my eyes and be back on the hill, sawbreathed, sodden with the wind, wiping the curses from my mouth.

The pretenders

'Paree' or 'Paris'? It's all well and good to round out your vowels, but conspicuous affectation when pronouncing foreign words is unforgivable.

I've just been in Kenya for a day. Flew there Monday, visited Tuesday, came home Wednesday. Even with my truncated attention span, I think this is pretty much my record. I was doing a story with a ferocious deadline. And here's the thing: although I spent more time travelling than being and doing, I have a voluminous collection of memories, insights, thoughts and experiences. Far more than a day's worth, like Mary Poppins's carpet bag, the trip doesn't seem to be able to fit into the time that was allotted to it. The intensity of the concentration needed to get everything seen and heard and committed to memory has made it high-definition.

I've always liked doing speed-tourism. Almost all travel-writing and foreign-correspondenting is about slow immersion, wallowing in your subject. It doesn't suit me. My senses grow soggy; I lose concentration, and the whole experience becomes panoramic, but with a softer focus. Arnold Bennett, the critic, was arguing about writing with someone who claimed superior knowledge because of 20 years' experience. No, replied Bennett, you have one year's experience repeated 19 times. Time on its own doesn't necessarily give you a concomitant increase in insight.

Anyway, that's not what I was going to talk about. I went to Kenya, the first syllable sounding like the thing that opens locks. My children, and everyone else, say Kenya, with the first syllable sounding like the Spanish word for 'what', which is probably technically politely correct. My way sounds colonial, but it's out of my mouth before I remember to flatten it; I don't say 'Injah' or 'Himaleeyas' with the last two syllables truncated into an English-swallowed abbreviation.

As a general rule of epiglottis, I think people have a perfect right to choose how they're known. If Bombay wants to be Mumbai, well and good. If Calcutta feels that the natty chic K of Kolkata suits its self-confidence, then it would be rude to cavil. I don't mind that they still sell Peking duck in Beijing or that Mumbai has Bombay University. I know that the capital of Greenland is Nuuk, not Godthab, and I wouldn't dream of calling Dunedin Edinburgh. I will make the best mouth I can out of the names people want to call themselves, though for liberal reasons I'm going to stick with Burma rather than Myanmar.

Winston Churchill made a feature of pronouncing foreign names with a pedantically English accent. Lyons was 'Lions', and Marseilles sounded like his mother was in a dinghy. I think this was done primarily to provoke the irascibly thin-skinned de Gaulle and appeal to Americans, many of whom think that foreign languages are the noise the devil makes. What I mind, and this may be ungracious and verbalist of me, is the other extreme, where names come with a boil-in-the-bag pronunciation. Or rather, I mind it inordinately, inappropriately, when people decide

to pronounce somewhere with a flavour of the accent of
the inhabitants, a lilting moue of polyglot garnish: an
Italian spin to San Gimignano, a curt German emphasis to
Bremerhaven, a Spanish lisp to Cadiz.

I don't just mind – it drives me to paroxysms of
murderous fury, which is made worse by the knowledge
that it's such a piddling small thing. It shouldn't
really bother me at all. It's so obviously an arrant little
affectation, like keeping first-class luggage tags on your
briefcase, or eating a banana with a knife and fork. But
despite myself, I wish nothing but foul and pestilentially
slow death on the loved ones of the offenders, and then
I want them in turn to be falsely accused of hideous
crimes of a disgusting nature involving farm animals, and
then be forced to live a life of mock-shame before going
sadly mad in great squalor and poverty.

I don't want to be irrational about this. What I mind is
the silly snobbery of those who add the inverted commas
and italics of a warmer tongue to their conversation to
imply some extra association or intellectual ownership
with the place. If I say Italian words with an Italian
accent they will correctly infer that I am no stranger to
southern climes. That I own a beret and can walk through
peasant markets squeezing produce with the insouciance
of a native. That I have canvas slip-ons with the heels
trodden down and can order from a simple bourgeois menu
without having to mime. This small inflection of mouthy
one-upmanship is meant to tell the rest of us of a whole
world of genteel, cosmopolitan, comfortably travelled
sophistication, when in fact it does just the opposite. It
reveals a cultural and intellectual insecurity and a brittle
narrowing of world views. It is only certain countries that
get the award of a music-hall accent. No one says Karachi

with the exaggerated Punjabi accent, or Ulaanbaatar in the manner of the Mongol. You don't catch the verbal tourist talking with a Yoruba accent. In fact, if they did, they'd be open to accusations of racist mimicry.

And that's the point. There is, in the pronunciation game, an implied league table of cultures, some of whom are worth imitating, and some who frankly aren't. So the old European countries get the nod of acceptance, and the developing world gets the mispronunciation of a purposeful snub. The kernel of what bothers me about this is that I suspect it's a peculiarly Anglo-Saxon affliction. Although I don't speak any other language well enough to know, I suspect that the French don't talk of Londres with a cockney twang, and Italians aren't referring to Birmingham by talking down their noses.

This geopolitical snobbery is just ours alone, and I'm collectively embarrassed. I expect Australians might wonder if they've made it into the English first division of Pommy mispronunciation. Well, funnily enough, I've recently noticed that both 'Sydney' and 'Melbourne' are being pronounced with a touch of open Aussie argot, but it's done with a sort of knowing ironic comedy, in the way people sometimes refer to 'Noo Yawk' and 'El Ay'. Americans, of course, are immune to all this because they pronounce everything wrong with gusto and utter certainty, and they should never ever be corrected. Imagining that Wooster sauce is actually pronounced 'Worcestershire' because that's what's written on the label is their prerogative. Far better and more honest to pronounce things in a way that suits your tongue than to pretend you have someone else's.

I once saw a chap sing the famous Fred Astaire song, 'Let's Call the Whole Thing Off'. He'd never heard anyone else sing it, so he read the words from the sheet music, and falteringly started, 'You say tomato, I say tomato. You say potato, I say potato. Tomato, tomato. Potato, potato' – I'm sorry, but what are you all laughing at? I don't think this is funny at all.

Big, bold Budapest

This Hungarian city has historically played second fiddle to Vienna, but Budapest has survived the misbegotten adventure of empire, and several wars, in better shape.

There is a rough old hitchhikers' rule of hitchhikers' thumb that if you want to get a really authentic feel for a country, go to the second city. I call it the Avis equation: they try harder. Second cities are always a bit chippy. Quick to take offence, bigger show-offs, faster to adopt new things, exploit the moment. Think Glasgow and Edinburgh, Milan and Rome, Siena and Florence, Bombay and New Delhi, Melbourne and Sydney, San Francisco and Los Angeles, Rio and São Paulo. It doesn't work everywhere. Birmingham is not the funky boutique alternative to London. There is no French city that comes close to Paris as a destination.

I just got back from a metropolis that has the biggest and most engaging case of Avis-itis in the world, Budapest. It started off as two cities separated by one-upmanship and the Danube. Buda is quiet, residential and ornamental. Pest is paprika, musical and monumental. You're probably trying to think what Hungary's first city is if Budapest is the second. Well, stop. Budapest is the only city in Hungary. There is another one called Szeged down

on the Serbian border, but by all accounts it's not worth
the bus fare. Budapest was the second city not of a country
but of an empire. The Habsburg Empire. They called it
the Austro-Hungarian Empire, but that was a bit like Pooh
and Piglet. The Hungarians got a severe dose of sibling
rivalry. Of all the people in the world, the ones you really
don't want to be patronised by in a confined space are the
Austrians. The Austrians themselves suffered from being
thought of as second-rate Germans and third-rate Italians.

Budapest did the thing that insecure siblings do to
draw attention to themselves. They built bigger and
bolder, dressed up brighter and fancier and played longer
and louder. The first thing you notice about Budapest is
the parliament. It is vast, and built in the Neo-Gothic
style. The architect went to London to look at the Houses
of Parliament for inspiration, and then thought, yes,
they're a start. We can do all of that, and add a dome.
If this is the mother of parliaments, then we'll build the
daddy. It is particularly impressive considering Hungary
hadn't governed itself for 400 years. Chucking up a great
Gothic pile like this is an act of stirring optimism or
ridiculous play-acting. The city boasts some of the most
attractive Baroque and Neo-Classical streets dotted with
Art Nouveau exhibitionism.

And now that all the bombast and bluster and vanity
and hubris of empire is gone, and Austria and Hungary
have both been shorn and stripped by two hot wars and
a cold one, they have both emerged straightened and
convoluted, obtuse leftover nations that seem to have
come through a long course of therapy. Austria is now
non-aligned but seems more neutered than neutral. It's
Hungary that has come through the misbegotten adventure
of empire in better shape. Smaller and poorer, but there's

a classy feel of hip cynicism and sophisticated expectation here. Vienna lives on nostalgia, politeness and mad dreams, but Budapest has that second-city ability to adapt, to exploit the new. It wears the past, which is almost all bloody bad, with an elegant, rueful grace. Vienna wears it like a shroud.

I wasn't expecting much from Budapest. Most people I asked said it was grey, cold, miserable and to eat before I went. Admittedly most of the people I asked were Viennese. I was lucky with the weather. It was bright and chilly, perfect for walking city streets. The cafés offer blankets so that you can sit outside till the last possible moment. I found excellent food. There is a beautiful central market inspired by Eiffel's engineers, a warehouse of glass and girders. Inside there is a nostril-humping collation of pickles, preserves, paprika and pastries. Hungary is a long way from any coast, and it's mostly a blasted steppe, so it's free from fish or green vegetables, which is such a relief. You can concentrate on the veal stew, the sour cream, the dumplings, the plums and cinnamon.

The city has a deep, abiding rhythm. Gypsy violinists lurk wherever two tables are gathered. The ancient syncopated extortionists of Middle Europe, they stalk the alleys of restaurants and cafés with the insouciant mission of mafia hit-men. I watched one large, gold-incisored grinning fiddler intimidate a Japanese tourist with lightning bow work flicked past the poor man's head like a samurai sword. His victim reached into his pocket and handed over his wallet. The violinist picked out three or four of the juiciest notes and bowed before shimmering off like a hungry shark, trailing Mendelssohn behind him.

I went to an afternoon concert in an Art Nouveau hall where Liszt had once played. The audience was immensely knowledgeable. There is a distinct pleasure in sharing music with people who know a lot more about it than you do. The orchestra knows it, they try harder and the conductor appreciates the applause more. And in the interval, they all trooped out and ate proper tiny opera sandwiches of smoked pig and hard cheese with gherkins and cocktail onions. I noticed that Joe Cocker was playing next month.

I'm haunted by Budapest now, its beauty, its sense of itself. Its café life, the music and the light on the Danube. In between Vienna and Budapest is Bratislava, the capital of Slovakia. It was closed. That's not a joke. Really, it was closed. I was there for two days, and everything I wanted to see, from the Jewish Museum to the Hall of Mirrors where the treaty after the Battle of Austerlitz was signed, to the UFO Restaurant, a hideous communist manifestation that hovers over the ugliest bridge in the world, everything was closed. It was caught in that malaise of disconnected inertia that's so often the legacy of communist countries. Places that sit and wait for someone to bulldoze them or give them a doughnut.

Bratislava has not got many tourists, but it does get the odd English stag party. My guide said that Slovakians tried to ignore them. 'The English are the worst. There was a bad incident. An Englishman masturbated into the fountain in the main square, in front of everybody.' Really? How awful. But I sort of know where he was coming from. You have to make your own entertainment in Bratislava, and hats off for managing to raise that much excitement.

Excess baggage

When it comes to travel, you are what you carry, or – more tellingly – what you leave behind.

One of the great mysteries of a traveller's life is why is it that the amount of luggage carried is in inverse proportion to the net worth of the traveller. The richest people travel with the least. The first-class queue is made up of passengers holding nothing more than a thin watch. Business, they'll be holding one of those hybrid cabin bags with a telescopic handle and detachable computer satchel. Tourist is made up of families and students shoving vast suitcases, like slaves building a Samsonite pyramid.

The most chaotic baggage hall I ever arrived at was Islamabad. The carousel was a revolving jumble sale, taller than a man. The wait and the exhaustion, the sitting in the frozen dark to get halfway around the world, had made most of the luggage give up the effort at being functional – it split its zips, broke straps, popped locks and vomited, eviscerated its contents into the steamy Pakistani afternoon. There were cooking pots and packets of spices and baby milk. Slithering intestines of wire that went with collapsed cardboard boxes and cheap electronics. Hair rollers, Teasmades, music centres and microwaves. There were the disembowelled paper parcels of meat. A collection of bar stools. Bundles of bras and big knickers. Children's nylon bedtime animals. All spinning past a crowd of shrieking,

shoving Pakistanis who were finally home after journeys
of tortuous inconvenience.

In the most basic markets in Africa, there is always
a stall selling large plastic carrier bags. They come in
either blue or green tartan and look as if they're made of
recycled twine. I work with a photographer who calls them
refugee Vuitton. You see them in every airport in the world
slumped in corners, lost and separated, often impounded
for the 101 infractions that are put there to stop the poor
from being poor anywhere but at home. These plastic
cases more than anything else mark them out as the
globe's slowest, most hopeful and fearful journeyers.

The answer to the conundrum, 'why do the rich have
least and the poor most', is that the rich travel with
nothing because they own everything. The poor travel
with everything because that's all they own. The rich
man gets what he needs at the other end. The poor leave
nothing behind.

I obsess about luggage, about bags and rucksacks,
money belts and secret pockets, steamer trunks and water-
tight compartments, camping equipment. When my flight
is delayed and I have to wait four hours, I while away the
time designing luggage in my head. In fact, I often try to
imagine my head as luggage and wonder if I can pack it
any more efficiently and what I'd leave behind if it didn't
fit in the overhead locker. Did you really need to take
detailed knowledge of a Peninsular war campaign and how
to skin and joint a rabbit to Malaysia? And you only need
one anecdote about prostitutes and diarrhoea.

I collect bags and smuggle them home. I have to
hide them. Usually I hide them in other bags. I have
an irrational fear of being separated from my bag in
transit. I only carry hand luggage. Hand luggage is in an

endless Darwinian war of attrition with people who man aeroplanes. It's a fight between passengers who want to carry as much as possible and an airline who wants to put as much as possible in the lost luggage pile at Schiphol.

I travel with another photographer who is equally exacting about packing. Most photographers are, because their kit is so delicate, provocative and plainly valuable. Once on a long flight of excruciating boredom we were whiling away the hours doing shadow packing and he said you've got to think outside the box. What do you mean? Well, what is a suitcase but a box. Think outside it. Outside it? It's laundry. Outside the box it's dirty washing. No, he said. What would you call a case with arms and a belt? You'd call it a coat. How many coats are you allowed to take onboard? I don't think there's a limit on coats. Exactly. Instead of thinking about small cases, we should consider bigger pockets. I reckon I could pack everything I need into a purpose-built coat.

He had a point. But wouldn't you mind being intimately and thoroughly searched by every customs officer in every flea-bitten airport we stop at? Because walking through customs wearing a lumpy duvet like the hunchback drug smuggler of Amsterdam may save you 20 minutes waiting by the carousel but it'll add an hour whilst rough men examine your secret places with a Maglite. But it's not a bad idea.

I have one bag that has been to pretty much every continent with me. It's leather, about the size of two rugby balls. It has a zip and handle and nothing clever or designed inside it. One thing you want to avoid in cases are designated or pre-assigned pockets and flaps, compartments. Think of a bag like a body and the stuff in it like organs. They keep themselves in place. I could

travel indefinitely out of this bag. It's like Noah's bag –
I take two of everything. Two trousers, two shirts, two
jackets, two pairs of shoes, two books. Usually I'm going
to countries that are hotter than London. Most places are.
And I can wash as I go.

I like everything to be the same. Identical shirts and
trousers and T-shirts. Every foreign correspondent I
know is in a constant search for the perfect travelling kit.
Exactly the right pair of trousers, the best shirt. Paring
down and adding up the multiples of use. We travel
with Tabasco and chewing gum and short-wave radios,
Moleskine notebook, space pen. Silk sleeping-bag liners
– essential for cheap hotels. A small light that will attach
to your head, a stash of dollars. The interesting things are
the small comforts that correspondents take. Comforts can
become incredibly important. I once travelled with a guy
who'd eat one jelly bean every night at 10 o'clock. He'd
just put it in his mouth and sit very still until it dissolved.
Personally I can't travel with pictures of my family – they
make me homesick and worried. But I always take a tiny
goosedown pillow, which squeezes into nothing.

And one of my books will always be Herodotus, the
father of history and travel writing. The collection of
observation, prejudice, analysis, lies, supposition and
brilliant colourful narrative, it has in it the essence and
joy of discovery. And although we're separated by two-
and-a-half millennia he reminds me of the purpose and the
excitement of travel. I also wonder what he travelled with.
What did Ancient Greek suitcases look like? You never
see them on the pottery or in the sculptures. They're never
standing there with suitcases or big packets of stuff tied
up with baler twine. There's never a man with a rucksack.
The Trojan War happened without suitcases.

The Swede life

Civilised and attractive, yes, but there's a contrariness at the heart of Sweden which is deeply alluring.

Paris in the spring, Gstaad in the snow, St Tropez in the sun, Roppongi in the dark. Everywhere has its season, its time. Except London. London only has one look. It's always London in the rain. For people from drier climes I know that sounds a bit like boasting, but I thought you might like to share a moment's precipitation porn because what's damply suicidal for me might be a bit of a wet dream for you. It's been incontinent here for weeks. Grey, feeble rain. Not strident, monsoonal, hard-arsed rain, but wimpy, prostate-dribbling double-wet fat drizzle, with the occasional bucket-load. Constantly. Everything's overflowing: gutters, rivers, cellars and a lot of homes in the south-west.

Still, like Florida cheerleaders, London looks best when wet. The glinting granite and Portland stone has a rubber beauty: streets of swaying umbrellas under yellow afternoon neon. The city doesn't look right in the sun. It's like seeing your gran on the beach. The new bits that are revealed you'd really rather wish weren't. But there is a lot to be said for visiting a place when you're not expected.

I think the most magical time to see Venice is actually in the autumn, when the tourists have left. The domes

and campaniles float in the mist, and the city becomes
a quiet, morbid and mysterious place. The sounds of
footsteps in alleys are muffled and there is the incipient
sense of ancient guilt and troubled secrets. I always like
seaside towns out of season. The gull-blown promenade,
the shuttered amusement arcade, the terminal depressives
walking sad dogs on the muddy strand, and old people in
plastic macs with thermoses in the shelters watching the
distant oil tankers.

By chance, I was once in Cannes when it snowed.
I was there in December. December in the south of France
can be beautiful. Chilly, but bright and clear. (In fact, the
worst time to be in the Côte d'Azur is in August. Not just
because everyone else in the world is there, but because
the air is muggy, thick and tastes like a million Germans'
bad breath.) I went to a restaurant on the quay, and when I
came out it had snowed and the whole town was pristinely
dusted with a fine layer, like a magic confectioner's final
touch. The Croisette sparkled, the palm trees looked
strangely biblical. It was a mixture of Victorian Holy Land
and gothic Christmas carol.

And in the streets ran a horde of shrieking, ecstatic
little North African boys. None of whom had ever seen
snow before. To see something this familiar in the
company of someone for whom it is astonishingly singular
is one of the small pleasures of the world. The icing on
the icing of the snow in Cannes was that only me and a
handful of Algerian boys were there to see it. And that's
the other thing about turning up out of season. Everyone
else has gone. If it had snowed during the film festival, it
would've been slush before it hit the ground.

I've just been to Stockholm. Now, everyone, even the
locals, said you should really come back in the summer

when it's hot and everyone's in the water in boats and canoes and you can swim if you're fast and hardy. Even in the summer it's still the Baltic. And they all go to merry little islands in the archipelago and sweat and eat herring in a hundred different ways in the never-setting sun. And have saunas and spend their summer naked without ever staring at each other's reproductive bits. That's when you should come, they said.

December is not yet white, but the sun is only let out, like a prisoner on death row, for a couple of hours. It's cold, and the wind whips off the water and ricochets through the narrow streets of the old town, eddying off the cobbles and buffeting the secure doors and shutters. But it's this very pearly grey light and the sprightly coldness of the pewter sea and the occasional moments of pale golden sun slanting off the windows that make this city in a country of 14 bite-sized islands so memorably enchanting in the sense of having come up and caught it unaware, resting. The place is at home with itself and the natives go about their pre-Christmas business with their collars up and their guards down.

Sweden and the Swedes are such a well-defined global brand. The capable hands that feel out the lie or the boast in inanimate things make beautiful design. The people who are in many ways a social paragon, the class swots at the top of the world. Like St Augustine, who prayed to God to make him good, but not yet, we might all aspire to be Swedish. But please, God, not yet. They all have a utilitarian beauty and a thoughtful, measured fairness. They care for the details of life. Every knife and fork is perfectly balanced. Clothes fit well and do their job with a sturdy confidence. Things have straight edges, their latches latch, their catches catch. It is the meeting of the worthy man-made with the smooth and efficient man who rarely sticks at the joints.

The Swedes are the form that follow function. But just under the surface is a bright, very uncool hand-knitted kitsch, a thigh-slapping land of peasant superstition and goblin folklore. Sweden's history is as hard, violent and unremitting as any in the world. Remarkably, they have created an enviably liberal state, but it sits like the crust on a pie. Scandinavians all seem to live with these binary contradictions. Empiricism with superstition. A sober rectitude and a fearsome drunkenness. Immense moral probity combined with a blush-making sexual liberty. There is a contrariness at the heart of Sweden that is deeply attractive. The balance of competing imperatives. It's their success in maintaining both without either overwhelming the other that makes Stockholm such a very civilised and attractive city. It's built on a human scale with human motives of trade, culture, inebriation, adventure and folk dancing.

I'm not making this sound like the most exciting place on earth. And it is a long way to go from almost anywhere you choose to get a lesson in civics. But it's often the subtlest harmonies that stay with you the longest. The taste of Stockholm lingers. A Swede told me the city was planning to get rid of all its petrol stations. Isn't that going to be jolly inconvenient, I asked. Well, a little, he admitted, but it's a precaution against terrorism. Petrol stations might be targets for suicide bombers. He looked surprised when I burst out laughing, mentioning perhaps Swedes were not top of Al Qaeda's devil-list. You think we're not worth blowing up, he asked, hurt. It was a very Swedish concern.

At last, supper

People love to talk about what they would eat for their last meal, but it's actually far more rewarding to consider one's favourite cuisine.

Two double-cheeseburgers, two large servings of French fries, half a gallon of vanilla fudge ripple ice-cream. Or perhaps cheese pizza, cheese omelette, green peppers and onions, white cake with white icing. Now these probably aren't anyone's choice for a last meal, ever – except they were for John Schmitt and David Dawson, two executed American murderers.

Reading through the last-meal requests from death row is one of the most gastronomically and socially depressing things you can do. I really don't recommend it. Rubbish food. Yards of enchiladas. Stacks of well-done steaks. Towers of pizza and buckets and buckets of fried chicken. Swimming pools of ice-cream, root beer, Coca-Cola and fruit juice. Tenements of pies and peach cobblers and vast ranges of chocolate cake.

Very occasionally you come across something out of the ordinary. Farley Matchett asked for four olives and wild-berry flavoured water. Arthur Rutherford had fried catfish and green tomatoes. Unusually for a last meal, he had it twice. The first time he was reprieved. The second time, not.

Philip Workman asked that a vegetarian pizza be delivered to a homeless person. The prison refused. On the day of his execution, Nashville's Rescue Mission received 170 pizza deliveries.

These meals are small windows into the lives that led to their consumption. Almost everything in them, you could get from convenience chains or diners. This is food without grace, without joy, without hospitality.

Johnathan Bryant Moore's life culminated in the self-inflicted dinner of Kraft cheese and macaroni and beef-flavoured Rice-A-Roni. Obviously, junk food doesn't necessarily make a drug-addled premeditated murderer, but it's an inescapable truth that with every last meal ordered at all executions over three years, not one of them was what you'd call home-cooked.

At the moment when a man might be expected to reach for comfort and a final taste of hearth and a family kitchen, something that his mother made, they only have franchised convenience food available. Almost all of it can be eaten with their fingers.

Only Sedley Alley, with an infantile pathos, asked for milk and oatmeal cookies. I was interested in this because 'What would your last meal be?' is one of the most common questions asked of food critics and chefs. Keen young home economists are always looking to turn out a celebrity cookbook of last suppers.

If your last supper includes something that isn't fried or you need to eat with a knife and fork and it doesn't come with ketchup or barbecue sauce or chilli, then it's almost certain you won't ever be asked to make the choice for real. Asking for a napkin to go with that would probably be grounds for a retrial. Bad food doesn't lead to bad lives, but rotten lives eat rotten dinners.

I always dodge the last-supper question because I think it's in bad taste. It's one of those things like 'Make up a list of the 10 sexiest women ever.' You have all the anxiety of the choice but none of the pleasure of the execution. You're never going to get a date with Uma Thurman and, in fact, your last meal will probably be an uneaten cold tomato soup.

Much more interesting from a foodie point of view is the question 'Which food would you choose for the rest of your life, if you had to live with one other people's national cuisine?' You can't choose your childhood food or a neighbour's that's too similar to make no odds. So if you're Irish, you can't say Scot. And you can't just say Italian because everybody just says Italian and there really isn't such a thing as Italian food: you have to specify a region.

I've thought about this a lot. In fact, sitting in airports and traffic jams and editorial pep talks, I think of little else. And I've got it down to four cuisines. Fourth is south-western France – foie gras and cassoulet, all sorts of duck, figs and roquefort. This is the home of the French anomaly. People here eat more saturated fat than anyone else on earth and have a very low incidence of heart disease. This is the food of old Gascony, of Cyrano de Bergerac: a cuisine for the last leg of life, of post-prandial naps, of meals that soak into each other, of a languid, replete and easy life. I could live with that.

In third place, there is the food of Piedmont, of northern Italy and the Po Valley, where they grow rice, make risottos, collect truffles, cook with butters, lard and the light olive oil of Genoa and have the youngest veal. I'd have to stretch it a bit to Parma, to take in hams, cheese and ice-cream, but that would do me. This is the origin of the Slow Food movement that grew to become

the Slow City movement and now has a slow university
where presumably they don't care much if you turn up for
lectures or not and you can take your exams over three or
four hours or perhaps three or four weeks.

Second is the food of the North West Frontier, the
mountainous tribal lands of northern Pakistan and
Afghanistan: the very best lamb curries, biryanis,
pilaus, apricots and quail, Peshawari naan, yoghurt
and pomegranate juice eaten with gusto and arguments
and your fingers on the roofs of mud-brick houses, in
a confusion of power lines and washing, the smell of
charcoal fires and the call of the muezzin.

And in first place is Vietnam. I love the food in
Vietnam. I love it so much I've invented new meals. It
is an ideal combination of delicacy and panache. It has
enormous variety of flavours and textures without being
irredeemably twee. It's refined but it's also assertive. It
has tiny little finger food and dog. But what really did it
for me was breakfast. When you consider a cuisine for
life, you have to start with breakfast. Your home style is
the most difficult thing to give up. I defy anyone but a
Japanese person to enjoy the breakfast of the rising sun.
My sub-continental Afghan breakfast of dhal, curry and
chapatti is difficult to swallow. Italians don't do much
more. They have a minute syrupy coffee and perhaps a bad
bun. But in Vietnam, they have a pho. The divine broth
with do-it-yourself additions of coriander, mint and chilli.
It's perfect. Actually, if you're going to have a perfect food
retirement, it would be Vietnam for breakfast, northern
Italy for lunch and then alternately south-west France and
the North West Frontier for dinner.

But if you want to start a real food fight, just ask
your next dinner table which of the three great staple

carbohydrates they would choose forever, to the exclusion of all others. Wheat, rice or corn, that is the decision that formed empires, made history and grew civilisation. So take your time.

For the love of money

- -

Muscovites have taken to
capitalism like pigs to swill.
You can see and feel the white-
hot energy of the free market, a
kind of economic Darwinism.

Here's a hypothetical question for those moments of
awkward silence in the pub: what would have happened
if, during the Cold War, Russia and America had changed
sides? When the dam of the Berlin Wall had come down
and capitalism flooded into the Soviet bloc like cold water
and drowned 100 million people in the unquenchable
desire for 50 varieties of doughnut, T-shirts advertising
Hard Rock Cafés in crap cities, reality TV and fantasy
porn, designer everything, and things that cost more if
given English names; what would have happened if, at the
same time, a wall had gone up on the 49th parallel and
along the Rio Grande and, overnight, America had become
a centralised command economy devoted to the promotion
of the common wheel and the negation of personal gain?
If all the shops had been full of the same suit and loaf
of bread, and if there was one television channel, one
newspaper and a thousand 19th-century classics in the
bookshops but no 20th-century ones. Who would've
coped better? In short, are some people more suited to
collectivism and some to individualism?

You may not think that a fair swap. You might think
that the point of the Cold War was not a struggle between
competing economic systems but a more romantic arm-
wrestle between good and bad, or perhaps right and wrong.
That's the assumption that most of us who grew up with the
phantom of choice and the scion of liberty believe. You
don't have to be any sort of ologist or an expert in isms to
know that the Americans would've been crap commies.
Not that they couldn't have managed all the authoritarian
secret police bits perfectly happily, or that they wouldn't
have gotten used to censorship and the absence of
adversarial politics in a week or two.

It's the working for the collective good that would've
stymied them. The land of entrepreneurial individualists
– where 'runner-up' is a long-winded way of saying
'loser' – simply wouldn't have been able to pull together
for no noticeable individual advantage. It's just not the
American way. The waves upon waves of immigrants who
went to America didn't make the gut-busting slog to be
team players.

I was in Moscow a couple of weeks ago and was
astonished at how naturally and enthusiastically they'd
taken to capitalism, like pigs to swill. You might
say, well, that's the nature of the free market. As P.J.
O'Rourke so neatly put it, capitalism is what people do
when you leave them alone. (Democracy, by the way,
isn't.) But that's not necessarily true. Many of the other
communist bloc countries have had real problems with
multiple choice. Albania, for instance, really didn't get
the hang of it, imagining that capitalism was some sort of
giant pyramid scheme with free money. The central Asian
'stans, Romania, Belarus, Ukraine and Moldova have all
had problems adjusting. But in Moscow you can see and

feel the white-hot energy of übercapitalism, a reductive
market fundamentalism.

I was shown around town by a rich, young entrepreneur
who had made a tidy fortune from dozens of businesses,
from frozen food to publishing to gas to restaurants, and
even a company that made $5000 ornamental fountain
pens. He'd started by importing Dutch shampoo and was
a millionaire within a year before he was 20. Moscow isn't
a pretty city, but it certainly is an impressive one. What
it lacks in looks it makes up for in power. It's not built
on a human scale. It's supposed to dwarf the individual
to proclaim the sovereignty of the masses, but now it
looks like the great barracks of Mammon. You can buy
everything, Dmitri told me with excitement. Everything
is for sale. You can buy a judge, a priest, drugs, women,
guns, caviar, children, a panda.

You can buy Boy George and Bill Clinton and the
Berlin Philharmonic and 500 Uzbek virgins for your
birthday party. You can buy silence and history and the
truth, and you can buy any rule, regulation or restriction
anyone else can come up with. This is capitalism. You can
buy anything, he said excitedly. What do you want? Girls?
Drugs? Food? Drink? Gold? A football team?

The story of competitive acquisition in Russia is
eye-bulging and heroic. The rich like to collect, but
they don't like to wait. So they buy lifetimes' expertise
in one week with one phone call. They have the largest
holdings of Ferraris or jukeboxes or small jade frogs with
ruby eyes. It doesn't matter; ownership is everything.
I realised a salutary truth: in Moscow, they understand
the lesson of capitalism, the true nature of the market,
in a way that we have never dared. It is unrestrained
economic Darwinism.

The press here is full of stories of foreign businesses being taken to the cleaners, fleeced, robbed down to their Calvins for not bribing enough, for not being frightening enough. The new Moscow marketeers laugh Slavicly: how stupid Western businessmen are. One of them I know went to a large Russian utility that he'd made a loan to, and owned a chunk of, and asked for his money back, as agreed in the contract. The Russians said no. They didn't say, no, sorry; no, maybe in a month; no, can we make a deal; or, no, the accountant's locked the chequebook in the desk and gone away for the weekend. They simply, boldly, unsmilingly said no, they wouldn't give him his money back. Because he wasn't big enough or strong enough to make them, and if he ever mentioned it again, they'd have his children killed. And, added the chairman, they'd use his money to do it. He went home.

Moscow airport is full of green-looking Western businessmen with white knuckles, holding back the tears because they have to go home and tell their boards and investors that they've lost the lot. And then they've got to go and tell their wives that they've got to sell the house, and try to explain this as a net gain because they've still got the kids.

Moscow capitalism is unencumbered by rules, aesthetics, manners, hypocrisy, taste and morals. It is the real thing: naked and toned, priapic and ravenous opportunism. Rich Muscovites have taken every Western excess and doubled it with amoral glee. The comforting snobberies and polite avaricious indulgences that took the West thousands of years to discover and refine are consumed and improved by Moscow's new entrepreneurs. Of course, all this two-fisted consumption only applies to a tiny epicurean sliver of Russia's population; the vast majority remain huddled in lives of relentless emptiness. There is precious little trickle-down. This is the truth about capitalism in its purest form: most people lose out so that a very few can overdose.

But they also seem to understand. When it was time for me to leave I fretted as ever about missing the plane. Moscow roads are gridlocked with the second-hand nicked motors of entrepreneurialism. Don't worry, said Dmitri, my driver will take you. Thanks, but he still has to use the same communist roads as everyone else. No, I've got a police car. How can you get a police car to take me to the airport? I'd buy one, he said, as if explaining an obvious and simple fact to a stupid child for the umpteenth time. Five hundred dollars to buy a police car – it takes you to the VIP lounge in the airport. Of course you can buy a police car. They're capitalists, too. The only Western snobbery that Moscow seems not to have taken on board is charity. I never heard the word mentioned once. All things considered, it would've been in bad taste.

Eye of the beholder

Recollection and emotion are inextricably linked. Even for a seasoned traveller, this means the most memorable views were captured by someone else.

A questing reporter has just asked me for my favourite view. Well, at the moment it would have to be that a woman's breasts are in direct inverse proportion to the size of her dog. I promise you, check it out: strange but true. Some sort of Darwinian deal, survival of the tittest. 'I'm sorry, you've misunderstood,' she said with an aridly unapologetic tone. 'What we want is your favourite vista. The view from the bridge, the window, the mountaintop.' Ah. Oh. Right. Yes.

I should've said, a tall blonde with four chihuahuas, but I didn't. I looked onward, and discovered with a shock that everything was black. Ah, I've gone retrospectively blind. I can't see a thing. Perhaps I've been robbed. My disc's been wiped. I can't remember anything I've ever seen. 'Oh dear. We're being a little overdramatic, aren't we?' No, honestly, my eye is empty. 'Perhaps you've just mislaid your album. Let me see. What about the Taj Mahal? You remember strolling through the garden, looking up at that majestic white dome, sitting on that little bench where the Princess of Wales was photographed? And Venice. You must've seen Venice, seen from the lagoon, rising out of the mist, the most romantic city in the world. And the Great Pyramid at Giza, you've seen that from the swaying back of a camel with the golden early dawn light and the muezzins' call to the devout?' Yes, yes, I like that. That's beautiful. 'Okay, so shall we put the pyramids down as your best view?' No, I've never seen the pyramids. 'You're being very annoying, you just said …' No, I said I liked the sound of that. I liked what you told me.

I added that I'd have to call her back after I'd had a think, and I've been putting off calling her back ever since. I have seen lots of miraculous things, I've seen Hong Kong from Kowloon. I've flown low over the Grand Canyon. I've stood on a mesa and looked out over the Navajo's painted desert. I've seen Mayan citadels on precipices in the rainforest. I've seen a humpback whale turn and regard me with a huge and mysterious eye off Cape Cod. I've seen herds of wildebeest streaming across the Serengeti. I've seen a coral reef thick with fish like the luxury Christmas sweetie selection. I've seen the Indian Ocean sparkle with phosphorus, and glow with a million iridescent jellyfish. I've seen autumn in the Appalachians, I've seen the summer night sky so clear that the shooting stars look like celestial taxis. I've seen lots and lots, from Cape Town to Reykjavik, and they were all amazing in one way or another, but they were not the thing.

I rarely travel with a camera. It's like picking and pressing wildflowers. A pressed flower is not an accurate memory of a living flower. An image of a place is not a re-creation of that place. Pictures owe more to other pictures than the thing they're of. The memory of the view of Hong Kong, for instance, leads me to the view of New York, and then of Rio. And I can't remember if the view I can remember is the one I saw or the postcard I bought or the magazine I flicked through last week. So I've been trying to attach feelings to pictures. I've been trying to remember moments of high emotion. Places and times, things that made me laugh or cry or gasp, and this is my top five, in no particular order:

- The waiter finally coming with a tray full of curry, when you're really, really hungry for a curry. This is a generic view because curry-hunger is like no other hunger. It's completely omnivorous. It's like gastro-demonic possession, foodie ebola. Sating it is the most important thing in your life for about five minutes.

- And then, actor Iain Cuthbertson. Now I understand that though he was a fine man, few people would think of Cuthbertson as one of their top five views. And it's only the faintest view of him, appearing through the steam as Jenny Agutter's father in *The Railway Children*. He has been the cause of more of my tears than any other view on earth.

- Waiting for someone who's late on a second date. I know there are all sorts of emotional, and frankly sticky sexual views you could put in here, but I think the second date is seminal. A first date is luck, charm, chardonnay. But the second is choice. And the beginning of something, and waiting for it is the most blissfully agonising moment. The sight of them coming through the door is … well, it's never that good again. That's the peg that all love affairs hang upon.

- Then your bag first on the carousel after a 12-hour flight. That's almost as good as the second date.

- Your name on a list: it's a great satisfaction to come across your name on a list. Obviously to find it on a

Colombian death-squad to-do list wouldn't be that great, but for most lists, from school teams to wedding dinner seating plans, there is a peculiar pleasure in being included in a crowd and finding yourself there. And the greatest list pleasure of all is finding yourself in a book index. Unless, of course, it's a book of war criminals.

But none of these will do for the lady travel editor, and I really have to say that the most incredible views of my life were, well, they were the Twin Towers coming down. We saw that how many times? Hundreds. Until the television stations agreed to stop showing it. And it never lost an atom of its shock. The Berlin Wall coming down. For my generation of Europeans, that was a defining – no, redefining – moment. Then that guy in Tiananmen Square, playing chicken with a tank. Kennedy dead. Diana dead. Martin Luther King dead. That Palestinian man trying to protect his son, dead. Churchill's funeral. Nelson Mandela walking out of jail.

You'll know most of these images. You could add as many again that I'd know. And in them, there is a salutary lesson for travellers and seekers of experience. The great moments, the burning images of our lives, are things we've never seen, and we are the first generation that ever lived who can say that. The greatest image, the best view ever, the most moving, awe-inspiring, memorable image was that most famous picture of earth-rise. It was so startling, so heavenly; none of us could know – how could we? – that the world was blue. How perfect. And it's still a view that none of us has actually seen. It only exists as a photograph and as a collective memory.

Behind the gloss

Italy, with its upside-down notions of vice and virtue, is truly spellbinding.

It was always said that the most brilliant piece of national PR was put about by the Austrians. They managed to convince the world that Hitler was German and that Beethoven was Austrian. That's very well, but still, nobody likes the Austrians very much. It's not as if you hear girls sighing, oh to be in Salzburg and meet a tall, dark choirmaster who'll teach me to waltz, and we'll have an idyllic life together breeding white horses that curtsey. No, Austria may have fiddled Adolf's passport, but it's still mostly zither music, boiled wool and the Von Trapp family to the rest of us. Ronald Reagan, during some White House junket, stood up when the band started playing 'Edelweiss', because he thought it was their national anthem, and to be perfectly honest, I thought it was, too.

No, for real global PR, the title of non-stick nation goes to Italy. Aww, I hear you say, as if looking at an orphaned puppy. Aww, Italy – what has it ever done wrong? Loads of girls sigh about wanting to meet a tall, dark Italian and doing anything he wants. What's Italy done wrong?

Well, forget Hitler – fascism found fertile ground in Italy. It invaded Ethiopia three years before the big war began. There, like most other colonisers, Italians committed cruelties. And then, when it was all over, everyone thought they were the victims. The Lombards invented interest rates, the Venetian Empire was venal and immoral, the Genoese were mercenaries. They may have given the world the Sistine Chapel, but syphilis took root in Naples. They could put that on travel posters, and we'd still flock there. After all, they said see Naples and die – and we went.

Italy has made itself into a looking-glass world, where none of the normal worldly rules apply. Take scooters. Only in Italy does a scooter look sexy and chic. And organised crime – everywhere else crime is a reason not to go; in Sicily, the mafia is an attraction.

Corruption. Everywhere else we call in the IMF; in Italy they call it family values. And northern Europeans, whose countries don't allow politicians to accept a doughnut, happily pay endless bribes to get electricity put into their holiday homes in Tuscany. And what's more, they feel happy and privileged to be allowed to join in the rustic corruption of Italian politics and pay the mayor.

Italy is a trough of special interests, fixing, foul play, pay-offs and excommunications. Italians wave their hands in mock exasperation, and the rest of the world smiles benignly, and goes, aww, those Italian scallywags. If Italy happened to be in the Middle East, there'd be a Yankee aircraft carrier in the Venice lagoon and sanctions. But Italians get away with it simply by being Italians, and we all know what they're like – and they know we know.

Every other nation in the world tries to make life be as it should be; the Italians make the most of how it is. We all say corruption is a bad thing; we must stop it. The Italians say we are all fallible; to pretend otherwise is arrogance. Everywhere else has crime, but in Italy, it's organised by professionals. All men are lecherous bastards who only want one thing; surely, say the Italians, it's better to be seduced by Casanova than Attila the Drunk. Instead of pitting virtue against vice in an eternal war of abstinence, failure and guilt like the rest of us, Italy has made the vices virtues, and vice versa.

If you come from a prescriptive, prudent, parsimonious society, this seems hypnotically attractive, and I am as mesmerised and seduced as any gap-year convent girl. Most years I try to find myself in Siena for the Palio. The Palio is a horserace held twice a year. But forget everything you know about horseracing. This isn't remotely like that. The Palio is unique to Siena, but it is symbolic of Italy. In the rest of the world, horseracing is organised along English lines. It is scrupulous, from the weight of jockeys to the piss of geldings; it is checked and fenced with rules. This, everyone agrees, is the only way to make racing fair.

The Sienese see things differently. Each area of the city, or *contrada*, has a horse, which they are given by lot. After that, anything goes. The horses are drugged, the jockeys are bribed and then rebribed and threatened. The horses gather behind a rope, except for one: they can only start running when he begins, and he will only start when he's been bribed by the other jockeys. This can take hours.

It's completely out in the open. The corruption is part of the event. Before the race, there is a splendid procession of *contradas* dressed in Renaissance costumes, throwing banners, marching in armour, and the great white Tuscan oxen pulling a cart bearing a banner of painted silk, known as the *palio*. Picasso made one; so did Matisse. Most of the great artists of the last 500 years have painted *palios*. This is all the winning *contrada* gets.

The preparations, parties, pageants, singing and arguments take a week. The race takes two minutes.

The victorious horse is carried to Siena's cathedral, where it's taken to the altar and a mass is said in its honour. Winning is the greatest moment in any *contrada's* life. The streets are full of weeping men; losing jockeys are beaten to within an inch of their lives. One, who fell off his horse in a suspect manner, had to be taken away in an ambulance. But the ambulance was stopped so they could get in and beat him up properly.

It all looks like a tourist spectacle, but it is ferociously local. No outsider can really understand the passion and the commitment of the Palio. This is a Siena thing. The most beautiful gothic city in existence is a series of dark circles that lead you to the heart of the greatest square in all Italy, which is to say in all the world. Walled in by Renaissance palaces, it hosts the race that is as corrupt and violent and hysterical and purposeless as it is searingly beautiful. Even to an outsider, it's poundingly exciting; but it is wholly and utterly woven into Siena and being Sienese. It is not like English horseracing or football or poker or basketball – a game that can be globalised. The Palio can only happen here, for people born in this dark, labyrinthine, ancient city. And in its bribery, doping, cruelty and violence, there is a pristine honesty. It is a race that is run not for highfalutin Olympian principles, but for the glory of the butcher, the baker and your neighbour.

Italy is complicated. It can only exist as long as the rest of us try to rise above our base natures. A world full of Italys would be a Dante-esque hell, but one Italy is a fabulous treat. As Orson Welles's Harry Lime in *The Third Man* famously pointed out: in 30 years of war, corruption and inhumanity under the Borgias, Italy came up with Leonardo, Michelangelo and the High Renaissance; in 500 years of peace, Switzerland produced the cuckoo clock. (And even that wasn't true; it was invented in Germany.) And remember where he said it: in Austria.

Burn for you

- -

The world is divided into those in the sun, and those out of it, and people in the shade will do anything to capture that little ray of sunshine.

There was something I was supposed to be writing about. A theme, some subject, that an editor somewhere distant told me would fit neatly, possibly elegantly, into this month's sybaritic world view. And I can't for the life of me remember what it was. That's not like me. Normally I'm diligent and industrious, acquiescent and compliant. But today isn't normal. Today is different. I can't remember, and what's more, I don't care. Whatever it was is a distant murmur, a carping echo. Today is different, and the main difference today is that I am hot.

Not that sort of hot. Not Californian-teenage-exclamatory hot. I'm sedately heated. The sun is on my back and for the first time in months I can feel myself pinkly burning. And it's so delicious, so radiant, it has driven all other thoughts from my head and I'm just enjoying the pearls of perspiration running down my back.

Have you noticed that hot and cold are both amnesiac? They have no memory. You can't conjure up the remembrance of temperatures past. The sun always comes as a blissful surprise, the cold a shivering shock. I've never had a first day in the heat when I haven't got

sunburnt. All these years I should've learned. I have
learned. I know that my pale, grey skin will blister
and peel. I know about carcinomas and freckles and
moles on stalks. But still, that first radiating burst is so
joyous. I can't tear myself away. The pain of tomorrow is
sufficient unto itself. This moment, I just want to point my
marmoreally adipose flesh at the sky for a taste.

You can cut the world across many different lines,
between haves and nots, first and third, buyers and
sellers, blondes and brunettes, tit-men and leg-men.
But sometimes I think the most fundamental division is
between those in the sun and those in the shade. If you
come from the dark, damp north, then the sun is always
joyous. A treat. Those who live in hot-and-bright all their
lives never really understand what fools the sun makes of
the rest of us.

The sad thing is that the favour doesn't work the other
way around. Going warm to chilly isn't an invigorating
pleasure. It's no accident that the lion's share of
humanity's innovations have come from places where
you want to spend as little time outside as possible.
It's not that cold, wet people are any cleverer than
warm, dry ones, it's that people with chilblains have the
greatest incentive to change things. We have to keep
active to keep the blood flowing. We have to invent to
keep our minds off the sleet and fog. A place in the sun,
a retirement somewhere with long blue shadows and
breakfast outside in a courtyard is the abiding spur and
dream of the north world. And much as we envy you, you
who wake up to gay Phoebus running his bright fingers
over your perspiring naked bodies, still also we pity you
a little. You are blasé with overexposure. Hot is the norm,
cold the shocking exception.

Where do people in hot countries go for a holiday? That's not a facetious question. We often think about it up here in February. Do you choose a different type of heat? Do you go from dry to humid? Do you count degrees? What's it like when all your holiday clothes are the same as your home clothes? You can never know the twinge of joy at meeting your favourite shorts once again after a year apart. The grains of last summer's sand in the pocket, the frisson of devil-may-care that a pair of sandals brings with them. Because, for us shadow people, the sun doesn't just turn us red and peeling, it is a licence. It brings out our other selves. Anyone who has had the misfortune of being around a breeding colony of young Brits on holidays will undoubtedly think that it's a side best left in the fridge.

But drinking, howling and ugly humping in the sun isn't all we do. It also inspires us to a sort of lyricism. A quiet, intellectual hedonism, a warm, grateful creativity that comes from our moments in the heat. How many great novels, films, songs, sonatas, paintings and poems are written by cold people who have found the light on their upturned faces? One of the most quixotic questions of global civilisation is, why did the cold world discover, conquer and colonise the hot one? Why didn't the Aztecs go and live in Germany? What was it that stopped the Thais from raiding Scandinavia? Why didn't the Mongols live in mortal fear of Egyptians? It is probably down to all sorts of things, technical, philosophical, capricious, but over all of them, there's the sun. Mad dogs and Englishmen are drawn to other people's middays.

Here's a statistic that will make you laugh: the incidences of skin cancer are almost exactly the same per capita in Britain as they are in Australia. I don't need to tell you that down in the southern hemisphere they've left the blinds open and all their exposed bits are being microwaved to a Chernobyl crispness. Whereas in Britain, the atmosphere is so opaquely thick, you often can't find the third floor, let alone the ozone layer. The sad, hopeless, touching reason for our high melanoma is that we've done it on purpose. We pay. In every poor, gritty, grey northern town in the country, in every parade of windblown shivering shops, there is a tanning parlour. A little place where, for a few quid, you can get radiated and come out looking like a posh spicy mandarin. And that's how much the sun means to us. We'll risk our lives just to have a brief memory, a warm reminder of holidays. Tanning beds are to the sun what pornography is to sex.

And that reminds me – what it was I was supposed to be writing about. Excellence. The best, the very finest, the thing that is without peer. Well, there you are: the sun. The greatest ever thing in the world. The best reason for travelling, the best reason for getting out of the house, out of your clothes and out of yourself. But if you wanted to say what was the very best way of serving yourself up to the sun, then that would be what I'm doing at the moment. I'm thinking of you whilst lying on the fantail of a perfect yacht that is slowly cruising down the Windward Isles and the Grenadines. As I speak, we're anchored off a deserted beach in front of a rainforest under a mountain in St Vincent. Exotic shoals of garfish are milling in the waters below. Above, frigate birds scissor the thermals and boobys dive elegantly for dinner. The sun is taking its bow, like a diva's gaudy encore, and it would all be utterly, utterly perfect if I wasn't the colour and texture of a flayed tomato, and stinging like a jellyfish massage. Out on the darkling shore, I can hear a mad dog somewhere laughing its head off.

Till death us do part

In Ghana, sending off a loved one in a personalised coffin is the last word in conspicuous consumption.

Before me as I write I have on my left a cup of congealing coffee and on my right the dog watching my grammar from her blanket in the soft chair. I press the random mix-it-up arrows on the iTunes and let the music go where it will, like some cheesy late-night DJ. I have the tonic breadth and the rhythmic girth of a man who really does know next to nothing about music. What that means is that, like a drunk on a street full of brothels, I'll jig about with pretty much anything. Which is why the first thing that's come on, just now, is Chopin's 'Sonata No. 2 in B-flat minor'. Only someone with musical taste so broad that it no longer counts as taste, but as more of a musical refugee, would have this on their work computer.

It's the one that starts with the piano – dum, dum, da dum – very slowly. It's actually the funeral march. The walk of black horses with plumes and men in top hats and bright carnations on, the coffin spelling out 'Monty, gone but not forgotten'. The tune that is to death what Mendelssohn is to brides. It's beautiful and lyrical, but also lachrymose, in a romantic sort of way. But like Christmas singles and summer novelty dance records, it's so branded by its associations you really can't listen to it just as music.

The reason I'm writing about it now rather than just listening to it out of the corner of my ear is because I was just about to write about the very thing it reminded me of. I was going to write about death. Actually, about coffins. And here, synchronously, like a premonition, I've got Chopin.

I've just come back from Ghana, which is celebrating 50 years of independence, the first colonial African country to be granted it. Today it's a very jolly place: 90-degree heat, 90-degree humidity. Everything grows here – plantains, cassavas, oranges, corn, malaria, elephantiasis, river blindness. Fence posts and wooden legs sprout. And there's cacao, Ghana's second largest export after gold. There's industrial diamonds. There's a toddler democracy and a hysterical press, and a lot of very scary, impressive women.

This is one of the best places in Africa, because its people are famously nice. Nice, funny, argumentative, loud, generous, inclusive and exceedingly competitive. Ghana has done well by African standards because Ghanaians care a lot about doing well, about getting on. They have a commercial streak you can skateboard over, and they like conspicuous consumption. They like the signs of wealth and success and education and state.

Ghanaians don't just wear their hearts on their sleeves but in repeat patterns all over their bodies. Clothes are made of bright fabrics that advertise everything from the national flag to a football team to your job. There's one that reads, 'I'll never get over a close family member who's just died', complete with skulls and coffins. You can have an insistent, jolly, anti-AIDS, safe-sex message on your new jacket involving broken hearts, kissing couples and ethereal haloed condoms. When someone dies, families take out exuberant, tearful death announcements in the newspapers. They also have T-shirts printed with 'Jojo, we'll never forget him; in our hearts forever', with a fetching picture of a beaming boy, himself in a T-shirt that says, 'You're beautiful and I've got the munchies'.

Nowhere are earthly status, achievement and dreams more vaingloriously celebrated than in death. Ghana is a very religious country going through an exclamatory low-church renewal. Good, godly people get on. God looks after those who love him. Poverty has no part in piousness here. Being poor in Africa isn't a sign of anything except that you're a poor African. Poverty is the default setting. So when you die, to show how well you did, how much God loved you by piling his bounty into your pockets, you throw a big funeral party with a lot of stew, chips and plenty of beer and a band, and everybody gets well and truly overindulged and remembers what a wonderful, kind, generous person you were – or, usually, what wonderful, kind, generous people your kids are for forking out for the funeral. Which is much the same as everywhere else in the world. What isn't the same is how you actually depart. Most of us can expect, at best, a box that looks like the top of a Victorian sideboard, lined with ruched silk underwear, going out dressed in a suit we resented like hell for having to put on when we were living.

But Ghana's developed the aspirational coffin. If you spent your life working in an office, they can bury you in a six-foot, smart black brogue painted to a shiny polish. Or you could have a sportier Nike trainer. You could get interred in a mobile phone, a lion, a spaceship. A castle. There's a spiny lobster, a Coca-Cola bottle. A snail. An anti-aircraft gun.

The showroom looks like a carousel ride of death, the coffins so beautifully made, Western interior decorators collect them as furniture. A gallery in California is putting on an exhibition. Which all seems a little disrespectful of the dead. A Ghanaian coffin has its origins in West African tribal masks, the animism of inanimate objects. It also has a touching and profound amusement, a thumbing of the nose at the ravages of mortality.

I almost ordered one for myself. They're all bespoke, unless you've always wanted to go as a Coke bottle or a Holy Bible. But what would I want to go in? What are my aspirations to eternity? I'm not as comfortable with my consumerism as most Ghanaians. I've grown up with it, not grown into it, so I'm not proud of my desire for a new ice-cream maker or a microwave. Certainly not proud enough to be buried in one. I don't want my family and friends' last sight of me to be a giant wooden Rolex or an Alessi teapot. I thought my coffin ought to be something related to what I've done in life. I work on a laptop, but I don't want to go in a Mac with broadband, or a big biro.

Then I thought, I write about travel for a living, and death is the last great eternal journey, so why not go in a suitcase with a label addressed to heaven and my name and dates stencilled on the top? And I was about to ask the undertaker how much it would cost to make me a carved wooden suitcase, and then I thought, actually, why not just use a suitcase as a suitcase? I'll be buried in a steamer trunk, like the one I took to boarding school. It's solid, it's green, it doesn't plagiarise someone else's culture, and it's appropriate. In the end, if I do feel a bit aspirationally Ghanaian about it, well, I can always go out in a Louis Vuitton one.

The anti-travel awards

The secret to a memorable life is judicious editing, and it's the same with travelling. Sometimes it's more important to know where not to go and what not to do.

Whilst travel writing may well be the best job in the world, writing for travel is one of the worst. Touring through Andalusia, eating at little local tavernas, is a joy; having to eat in every taverna in Andalusia would be a Spanish Inquisition of rare cruelty. The secret to an exciting, accomplished and memorable life is judicious editing. It's essential when you're travelling. The most important decisions are what you choose not to do, not to see, not to eat, not to pack and not to get tattooed on your backside. The pitiful guidebook hack has to do it all. Every last slummy nightclub and sticky internet caff, every lodging house and campsite, and every bus terminal and puppet theatre, so that others who come after don't have to.

Guidebook writing sounds like a blessing but is, in fact, a curse. The writing rarely rises above the level of an instruction manual. It's a constant headache of opening times, addresses and directions. The pay is negligible, the expenses frugal and you're not allowed to accept freebies or bribes. When I travel, the first thing I say is, 'I'm the man from *Australian Gourmet Traveller*, bring on the dancing girls and the cornucopia of largesse.'

At last, a guidebook author named Thomas Kohnstamm has written a memoir called *Do Travel Writers Go to Hell?* about his days writing for Lonely Planet. He specialised in Latin America, apparently, and what with the lack of cash and the slimness of the deadlines and, presumably, the largeness of the countries and the shittiness of the roads, he apparently sold drugs, gave glowing reviews to restaurants whose waitresses slept with him, plagiarised other guides and, best of all, wrote part of one for Colombia without ever having gone to the country.

Now here's the thing: I'm immediately more interested in reading the imaginary tour of Colombia than I am in any actual plodding been-there-done-that guide. In fact, I'd rather read a magic-realism introduction to Latin America written by Finns who'd never left Scandinavia. There's definitely a niche market for fantasy tourism. They always say it is better to travel hopefully.

The other guide I'd really like to have is '100 Things You Thought You Wanted To Do But You Really Shouldn't Bother'. Travel writing always starts off with the tacitly agreed assumption that whatever place you're looking at is one of the best, friendliest, most exciting, rewarding, beautiful places on earth, with charmingly friendly people, memorably delicious food and indigenous handicrafts that will grace your home and body forever. And, of course, it can't be true of everywhere. Some places and things have to be disappointing. It would be really useful if someone would write and tell us where they are. So let me kick off with my 'Top Nine':

1. *The Silk Route.*
   Sounds like the most romantic destination in the world: the great trade route that stretches from China to

Constantinople. In fact, Central Asia is a catastrophe of
soil erosion, pollution, autocratic totalitarianism, police
states, poverty, disease, growing Islamic militancy,
and some of the most mistrustful, taciturn people you
could hope to meet. Places like Samarkand, Bukhara
and Tashkent have the ring of Arabian Nights romance
about them, but actually they're decaying slums of
Stalinist architecture built to intimidate subjugated
people, with occasional stunning 10th-century
buildings that just remind you how ghastly everything
else is. And the food is inedible.

2. *Gondola rides.*
The minute you gingerly step into these gay canoes,
you know it's a mistake. First, there's the unsmiling
oarsman who looks like a cross between a pork butcher
and a French mime and is, in fact, a member of one
of the most vicious closed shops in Europe. He will
precariously punt you up the narrow ditches that are
Venice's canals. You will be serenaded by a stream of
gothic curses and threats as he bellows at the other
denizens pushing tourists up and down. Being so much
closer to the water, you can get a much better smell
of Venice's effluent and while you can't see anything,
everyone on the bridges can see you. They'll stare
and think, 'Isn't that bloke too fat to be afloat?' It'll
cost more than everything else you do in Venice put
together, and all the above also applies to gondolas
in Vegas.

3. *All the rest of Las Vegas.*
I'm not going to argue with you about this. Las Vegas is
possibly the worst man-made thing in the world.

4. *Camel rides.*

Don't ride the camel anywhere, ever. If you do get
bullied into sitting on one, resist the urge to shout:
'Onward to Aqaba; no mercy, no mercy!' Every camel-
owner has heard every single Lawrence of Arabia
joke, and none of them have seen the film. There is
one overwhelming reason why you should never ride a
camel: they don't want you to. Camels hate you. Much
the same goes for elephants. Once a year, an elephant
goes mad, reaches back with his nose, grabs a pink
tourist and throws him to the ground before stamping
on him. Don't ride the donkeys down the Grand Canyon,
or the horse-drawn carriages around Central Park.

5. *Swedish massage in Sweden.*

It's a huge disappointment. You imagine something
Swedish, liberal and erotic performed by Anita Ekberg.
In fact, it's a massage done by the woman from the
kitchen appliance department of Ikea, and it really isn't
site-specific. It's much the same as a Belgian massage.

6. *Whale-watching.*

Smelly, noisy boats with a constant tannoy, chugging
about trying to find immensely boring fish that look like
badly folded mattresses. All they do is swim aimlessly.
Worse than the whales are the other people on the boat
with you. A pitiful collection of homespun hobbits
who will bellow tearfully at the water and be moved to
ecstasy, and you're going to be stuck with them for
four hours.

7. *Turkish massage in Turkey.*

If you want to know what it's like to be covered in soap

suds and become the sexual kebab play thing of a 16-stone man with a back that's hairier than a Polish folk festival then, by all means, give it a go.

8. *Railway journeys that take longer than one night or two meals.*
Yes, it sounds romantic and authentic. In reality, it's like being trapped in a horizontal lift with 15 consumptives and an open sewer. Ask yourself: which long-distance train journey would you make in your own country for fun? So why do you think it's going to be that much better in someone else's?

9. *Greece.*

Entry denied

*After years of persecution, the
Roma – or Gypsies – are still
here and still suffering the
implacable racism of
middle Europe.*

I'm back in France and this column's very late. Very, very
late. If you're reading this, it's a small miracle of speed,
typing and the printer's inky art. I forgot I was supposed
to be in France again this summer, and then the bags
appeared in the bedroom and I said, 'Hey, where are you
going?' and she said, 'We're going to France on Monday.'

'I've got a lot of writing to do.'

'Well, you can do it there.'

So I felt a little lighter, a little jollier, for the rest
of the day because that's what France does to you. The
happy surprise that in two days I'd be in Provence played
a petite accordion in my soul. All over the world it's the
same. Statements that you're going to France on Monday
turn the brain to croque monsieur. And the odd thing is
that the pleasure of knowing you'll be in France is in no
way mitigated or spoilt by the knowledge that you'll be
surrounded by French people.

So here I am. I'm not going to bore you again with a
middle-aged Englishman's maunderings at the joys of the
vie artisanal. I'm sitting in the sun by the pool, smelling
like an abused coconut, my cheeks sticky with warm fig

seeds. I'm not actually thinking I'm here. I'm somewhere
further north and east.

A couple of years ago I made a journey along the
Danube, starting in the Black Forest and ending at the
Black Sea. I must have mentioned it – it was a memorable
and resonant trip. I loved it as much as I've loved
anywhere I've been. It was the story of Mitteleuropa, the
heart of Europe, written in water. I finished with a sob
of violins.

When I got to Constanta in Romania on the Black
Sea coast there was a ruined and abandoned synagogue,
and I realised that all the way down the river there had
been synagogues that were now cultural centres or Jewish
museums. There were Jüdenstrasses and the distinctive
spices and baking of Jewish cuisine. There was plenty of
evidence of Jews and Jewishness. There just weren't any
people – not the Jewish people. The Danube had been
their river; the river of Jews. They had traded up and
down it, and every city on its banks had had large Jewish
populations. But no more; they had been wiped away.
The Jews of the Danube were dust and ashes, or they
lived as the Jews of Tel Aviv, the Jews of New York and
London, Buenos Aires and Melbourne. But here they
were ghosts, ripples on the water, a sigh in the lapping of
an ancient dock.

I filed the piece and it went to press. It was okay, but
I realised there was another story I hadn't told because
I hadn't had the space. If I'd started, it would have been
another 1000 words, and it was contentious, current and
political. The other story of the Danube is the story of the
Roma – the Gypsies. They shared the same unthinkable
persecution as the Jews, died alongside them in the same
camps, were exterminated and displaced. But they didn't

disappear – they're still here and they're still suffering the implacable racism of middle Europe.

The greatest number of Romanies are in Romania, and they live a separate, apartheid life. They have their own language and food and the women dress differently. And the Romanians talk openly and easily about how dreadful they are; they vilify them with a comforting familiarity. The racism, the distaste, the disgust at Gypsies floats through Europe like a secret, intimate sexual infection; everyone has it but no one talks about it to strangers. In Hungary, Gypsies are beaten and burnt out of their homes. When Czechoslovakia split amicably in the Velvet Revolution between the Czech Republic and Slovakia, they divided the army, the gas board, the post office and the ornithology club, but neither nation wanted to take responsibility for their Gypsies. In Vienna, the Austrians add Gypsies to the already overcrowded list of their prejudices.

Through all of Europe, Gypsies are denied education, health care, employment benefits, housing benefits. They live outside official systems. They're prevented from getting insurance. They can't run businesses or get loans or credit. The Gypsies are forced to work outside the law; they are universally believed to be endemic recidivist criminals, and so often intolerance creates the conditions to prove itself right.

I'm thinking about all this because, here in France, the Gypsies are being deported en masse back to Romania. Once more, trains of unwanted untermensch are being trundled across Europe. These people, identified by their racial origin, are asked to account for themselves because of some eugenic code that says they were born to be criminals, to be a burden, to be a stain on a civilised country.

There's precious little fuss being made. Hardly any other Europeans stand up to be counted with these dispossessed. Any criticism is mostly from people who want to score points off Sarkozy. The Romanians are a disposable stick to beat the president with; precious few are shouting, 'How can this be?'

How swiftly we forget. How can a nation that has had its own citizens shipped east so easily and glibly do it to others, to these fellow Europeans who have shared this continent with the rest of us for millennia? Here in the south of France, in the flat fields of bulls and white horses, the picturesque version of the Gypsies and Gypsy life is a tourist attraction, a cultural treasure – their guitar music, their songs, the bright patterns of their cloth. In Spain they dance; in Hungary it is their haunting violin.

Gypsies have a fugitive culture. If it came from anywhere else in the world Europeans would be holding charity dinners and forming committees to defend it. But now the nation that with such vaunting pride proclaims itself the birthplace of liberty, fraternity and equality is transporting the most needy and persecuted minority in the European continent. Although the Gypsies shared the same status as Jews during the Holocaust, no one ever called for a Roma homeland because nobody believed they would ever need one. Why would they? They belonged here with us in the most civilised continent in the world. From Donegal to Andalusia, Gypsies were one of us. Their problems were Europe's problems; their music, our song.

Obviously not. This is all beyond shame, beyond dishonour. But it isn't beyond the warning of memory. This is how it begins.

Sorry, this isn't what I was supposed to be writing about; it's probably not what they wanted.

Revel without a cause

*The problem with extravagant
shindigs and elaborate children's
parties is that they're attempts
to manufacture happiness – and
happiness never sends
out invitations.*

There is a cocktail-stick rule of entertaining that I think
can be found in an appendix of Newton's *Principia
Mathematica*, or perhaps it's a footnote in the Book of
Revelation, that parties are great in inverse proportion to
the time, effort and money that are allocated to them. A
party is a collection of random and extemporal moments
that somehow collide to make a collage that turns out the
next morning to have had a plot: a beginning, a middle and
a happy ending. Planning a party is like setting a trap for
mist: the more elaborate and diverse, the more impressive
and ostentatious the decoration and the lighting, the more
baroque the bait of entertainment, the lure of cocktails
and wine fountains and spitted hogs, the more you notice
the absence and the will-o'-the-wisp that is that magic that
makes a party.

The most extravagant and elaborate bash I ever went
to took a year to plan, a Third World debt to pay for, and
the imagination of at least three Oscar winners. It was
costumed and pyrotechnicked to within a couple of feet of
God. Every possible wish, whim and spoilt demand was

catered for, from midgets carrying silver trays of coke, to
bunny girls offering Cohibas and champagne. There were
chill rooms and dance floors, banquettes and bars, pools
and fairgrounds, benches, armchairs, divans, waterbeds,
li-los and a rack. As we the guests turned up, exhausted
with expectation and the gorgeousness of our costumes,
we just stood in awe, struck mute and shy by the grandeur
and the brutal excess. We traipsed around the party
whispering, like prospective buyers being shown around
a house that we knew we couldn't afford. The largesse was
so overwhelming that we'd all gone home by 11.30pm,
defeated by our own failure to rise to this occasion.

Contrarily, the best party I've been to was decorated
by a fire on a beach. It wasn't meant to be a party at all.
There were no invitations, no dressing up, a couple of
bottles, some lobsters, a cappella singing, and the vast
Milky Way by way of fireworks. Come to think of it, all
the best parties are decorated by fires, that circle of
light, Promethean and elemental, the connection and
the community made by fire, the ring of warmth in the
chill. But because I live in the middle of a city, and
serendipitous bonfires are frowned upon, I don't throw
many parties. I find more than half a dozen of my friends
in a room confusing and rather depressing.

But because latterly I've become a father again, I'm
now flung back into that strange fun of children's parties.
There is a list of all the things that I'd forgotten about
kiddie get-togethers. And the first item right at the top, in
caps, underlined, with exclamation marks, is: children's
parties are not fun. They're not at all fun. They're not at
all fun for anyone. I'm talking about parties for the under-
fives, you understand. For little kids. Little kids' parties
are high-stress events. The children made to wear weird

stuff. They don't know what's expected of them. They have to share food with strangers. Their cosy, comfy safe houses are full of people they don't know. The furniture's moved around. Then either some other little moppet is getting all the attention, which is worrying – maybe this is a competition and mummy's going to take the new one home – or they're getting all the attention, which is terrifying. Other grown-ups are coming up and kissing you and they've set your dessert on fire and then they chant some sort of curse and it's the worst day of your life. So you have hysterics and regurgitate and your mother hates you for ruining whatever it was this was supposed to be. For most children, their first birthday party is their first social humiliation. This is where we all learn what to expect from our lives.

What bothers me more than the obvious misery and insecurity parties are going to inflict on my kids is the desperate misery and insecurity they're going to inflict on me by proxy. There is some weird, and frankly unfair, genetic amplifier that turns up the pain of life through your children. If I lose a race (this is hypothetical, the chances of me racing anything or anyone are nil), I go 'Ho-hum, I've lost a race', I'm really not that bothered. But if my small child loses so much as a sack race, I know it'll be a sickening blow that'll feel like a high velocity bullet. The only thing worse than your own birthday party is your child's birthday party. An infant human's natural instinct is to burst into tears when confronted with a flaming cake and a clown.

We have to be taught to like parties like you have to learn against your better instincts to enjoy smoking and hard liquor. It's no coincidence that all these things come wrapped up in the party bag. I used to hire a children's

entertainer called Naughty Nigel, or perhaps he was called
Evil Edwin or Recidivist Richard. He was a paragon of his
calling, a balding, sad, half-cut, thwarted, ill-tempered
loner who incubated a Sahara of dandruff and had teeth
that reminded you of a komodo dragon. Through long
experience of kids he'd grown to loathe them, almost
as much as he loathed parents for having kids. His act
never varied. He was never surprising, or entertaining,
or original. The children sat cross-legged watching him
with a wary moribund concentration, because children
will look at anything with a wary concentration: fish
tanks, Spongebob Squarepants, their parents having sex.
They always resisted Pedo Pat's encouragement to join
in – again it's hardwired into our DNA that audience
participation never led to any good. The birthday child
had to be bullied and dragged, whimpering and shivering,
into the spotlight for the clown to give him or her the
prize. In Naughty Nigel's case, this was always the same:
from an apparently empty box he would produce a terrified
chinchilla, which was obviously as thrilled to see another
child as the child was entranced to be presented with a
surprise rat made out of fairy floss.

There was a moment when the children made it to
eight or nine that they'd start abusing the clown, throwing
things, telling him they could see the bunch of plastic
flowers up his sleeve or threatening to call social services
if he got any closer. And at this point you knew as a parent
that their party training was over. They could go on with
the rest of lifelong expectations and disappointment and
mass entertainment.

The best of parties is the morning after. The hungover
brunch. The restorative Bloody Mary. The post-mortem.
The dissection of the goodtime corpse. Parties, like saints,

are nice to remember but hell to live with. Parties are hubris. They're an attempt to manufacture happiness, and the lesson of life is that happiness is fleeting and random, and happens despite our best intentions, and never ever sends out invitations.

Danger becomes you

If life's getting too much, forget pampering, take an unrest holiday instead.

Adam and Eve were the first refugees. The first people ever were the first asylum seekers. Where do you go for help when you're the only people on earth? You can't even pray. You can imagine the sort of reception they'd have got today: 'So you want to claim political asylum, and you're from Eden? We don't have any reports of unrest in Eden; the Department of Foreign Affairs and Trade has designated Eden as paradise. You say there was this angel with a fiery sword who came and threw you out. Could this have been a political police angel? No? Okay, it was a religious fundamentalist angel. What was your offence? Nicking an apple. Anything else? I don't care if it is embarrassing, love, it's gotta go on the form. Knowledge. What sort of knowledge? Carnal knowledge. It was the first time? Well, everyone has to have a first time. Oh? This was the first time ever for anyone? Right. And you got prosecuted and evicted for having sex in public? Okay, so there wasn't any "private". Would you mind telling me why you're not wearing any clothes? Because you didn't know you'd be needing any until you got kicked out? I don't want to be disrespectful to your beliefs or anything, but it doesn't sound like much of a paradise to me.'

The Bible is a litany of refugees, flights and wanderings. The Old Testament is the first collection of travel writing, and it's all disastrous. Wilderness, 40 days of walking in circles, despair and distant horizons, thwarted dreams, ruing, locusts and honey. And the flood: the ark is the first cruise ship. The journey is the plot and instigation of a lot of religion. All those trips stand as a metaphor for our life journey. The ancient need to go on a pilgrimage seems almost universal, from Aboriginal walkabouts to Santiago de Compostela and the annual hajj to Mecca. Travelling to discover things about ourselves is the oldest exploration, as old as travelling to escape the truth of others.

I've been thinking about all this because I've just been back to the Garden of Eden to see what the old place is like. You know it's had some changes. The original Garden of Eden – in fact, the original concept of all gardens – is Babylon, the land between the Tigris and the Euphrates. Today, there is nowhere like Eden left in Baghdad. If you wanted to draw a strictly biblical fable to show why we got chucked out in the first place, then the state of Iraq today would be a pretty good illustration.

Baghdad was frightening. Not in a car-crash sort of way, more in a sustained horror-movie way. It's the suspense, waiting and watching. You know that all the time you're moving in a space between explosions, and everyone's life here is caught in the parenthesis of someone else's death. But it is, at the same time, very exciting. And that excitement is like a guilty secret we carry around inside our body armour; we know we really shouldn't feel anything like pleasure at visiting here.

Perceived and real danger does appeal. It takes away the veil of your senses, the prophylactic of living in a country at a time when your safety is someone else's responsibility. Where you can rest easy, smug in the knowledge that there are armies of health and safety professionals who never cease to work at your well-being, making sure that your world has guardrails and safety caps, that if you fall over, someone will be there to pick you up and maybe even give you a little reward.

There is an elation in knowing that you're living on your own recognisance and that you are an uninsurable risk. Of course, I was surrounded by a lot of soldiers with guns, but we all shared a real and present danger. And one of the pleasures of danger is that it seems to add a precision to your eyesight and a clarity to your hearing. Driving through Baghdad, the panorama of gritty, packed streets and twisted, burnt cars becomes pin-sharp. Every face is examined with a forensic care. There is a heightened awareness to everything.

When I flew low over the city in an old Puma helicopter originally built by blokes with quiffs and brown overalls who were listening to Gerry & the Pacemakers on the wireless. I sat inside the door beside the machine-gunner and watched the ground slide away beneath us as we zipped over the poor streets, and I realised I was concentrating on the journey, looking at it so hard that I can now re-run it like a movie.

I've taken loads of hops in helicopters, looked at millions of streets, seen uncountable things, but they swim together into a soup of memory. Few things are photographically memorable, unless they come with an equally strong emotion. A thing being beautiful or big or small or bright or unusual isn't enough. It needs the label and the wrapping of a feeling to fix it. I remember the first time I saw the girl I live with as if the moment was set in crystal. I can recall every minute detail of the only man I've ever seen killed, and l wish l couldn't.

And when I returned home, the emotion and the feeling illuminated the picture of this latest experience. Coming back from Baghdad had an intensity that was reflected in walking in through my own front door and putting on the kettle, patting the dog, going to look at the garden. I finally learnt a lesson that had been slapping me in the face for ages. Our continual hunt for relaxation – de-stressing, chilling, hammock-swinging, pool-schmoozing – is all wrong. We think that we want to give ourselves a break, and there is a huge pampering industry geared to arranging this for us. It'll switch down the volume and remove the sharp edges, serve everything tepid and soft, take away the decisions and the cares. And it's all the wrong way around.

What we need, what makes us excited and active and interesting, is the danger and the self-reliance. If things are getting on top of you, what you need is an unrest holiday. You need more and different stress, not less. Relaxation is breathing out. The good bit is taking a deep breath and jumping in. I've finally understood that getting chucked out of Eden is the best thing that ever happened to us. Without that, there would be no story, no adventure. And the sex is a bit of a bonus, too.

Glazed and confused

---

*God gave his only son, England
gave tinsel and figgy pudding –
Christmas is a fine time to
skip town.*

The English gave much to the world. Runny noses,
sensible shoes, short vowels and baseless condescension.
All these are known and loved around the globe, but
perhaps England's greatest gift is unattributed and goes
unthanked. It was England that gave you Christmas,
with the recipe in the pocket and the strict caveat that
if it didn't fit, you could always take it back for another
festival. Before you put up your hand and swear that the
vicar said God gave us Christmas, well, yes, technically.
But he also gave us diphtheria, toe jam, easy-listening
music and England.

Everything you know and associate with Christmas
was actually an invention of the English. To be strictly
fair, by two of them: Charles Dickens and Prince Albert.
From them we get fir trees, holly, ivy, geese, turkeys,
crackers, puddings, cards, families and guilt. Again,
some of the more pedantic of you may be aching to
point out that fir trees and carols and indeed Albert are
German. And again, technically, you have a point. But
the essence of Christmas, that peculiar paper-hatted,
sated melancholy that descends in the afternoon of the
25th – that is peculiarly English. That and the deep,
nameless feeling of disappointment and longing that

wells up when you finally unwrap the last present. That's uniquely English.

As is the festive meal that involves a collection of ingredients no sane chef would ever construct, including three dishes – cake, pudding and pie – made with identical confections of dried fruit. As a young food writer, I was once asked by a magazine editor to come up with alternatives to turkey, figgy pudding and the rest. 'Tell me about Christmas from other cultures,' she enthused. (I now know the hunt for the alternative Christmas feature is as traditional as Fair Isle sweaters.) Anyway, I dutifully wrote of oysters in France, pig's foot sausage in Italy, carp in Czechoslovakia, goose from the Carpathians, and the peculiar and weird, boiled, year-old skate from Iceland. I was called into the office.

'This isn't good enough, is it? It's too predictable. What do they eat for Christmas in India, or Vietnam, or, I don't know, Saudi Arabia?' Inwardly I sneered at the parochial assumption that Christmas was international, and went away anyway and made up stuff about festive palm trees hung with sparkling sheep's eyeballs.

But then one year the person over the other side of the Christmas table said, 'Why don't we go somewhere hot for Christmas?' You mean just after Christmas? 'No, for Christmas.' Oh, I couldn't. It's not possible. I think there's a law – you have to stay at home over Christmas to do all that stuff. 'What stuff?' Well, complain mostly, about the weather, and the amount of junk in the shops. About how the Christmas lights aren't what they used to be. About the amount of work for just one day. About the meanness of your family, and the appalling manners of mine. About the ghastly decorative pollution of Christmas cards, the vomitous kitsch of seasonal television, and mostly about how out of control the commercialism and feeding-frenzy greed of the whole damn down-the-chimney business has become.

'Why don't we go somewhere else?' Well, I don't know, really. But I have a suspicion it would be like running away. 'Exactly.' So we ran. To the Caribbean. I approached the beach on Christmas morning like a man who had just joined a weird and shameful sect: nudist cross-dressers, conversational Esperanto users. But there was also, buried in the naughtiness, a feeling of lightness, of a load lifted, as if I'd lost my parents' luggage accidentally on purpose. We sat on the beach, ate salad for lunch, feigned other-worldly indifference when thonged Germans muttered seasonal greetings.

I thought I'd got away with it, until Father Christmas turned up on a jet ski, an absurd puce Englishman in a woollen cape, wellington boots and a stick-on beard, being driven by a semi-naked Rastafarian who couldn't contain his howls of derisive laughter. Santa stumbled ashore and handed out plastic hairclips and water pistols. It was then I realised the full impact of the global ho-ho-ho warming that is the English Christmas. It was a cathartic moment.

Since then, I have never spent a Christmas in England. I have gone to further and greater lengths to avoid any festive hint or tinsel. Not because I mind terribly, but because I want to know if there's a single corner of the globe that's Dickensless or Albert-free. So far, I've failed. In Goa, blaring Hindi renditions of 'Jingle Bells' over loudspeakers. In Thailand, plastic holly in cocktails, Santa on a gold-painted elephant, and mince-pie pancakes.

I actually thought I'd cracked it in the Kalahari. This is the least commercial place on earth. If Mary had sprogged in the open here, Christianity would have bought the farm before it was two days old. But I came back to my fly-camp to find an acacia tree covered in candles, put up by a cook called Adolph who thought I might feel homesick. He also turned out to be born-again, and rather movingly shared his Bible and prayers with me.

Oddly perhaps, the place I've found with the least Christmas is actually the neighbours upstairs, Scotland. We don't go in for it up north. It's England's thing. We save ourselves for the grander, more ancient festival of Hogmanay. New Year is pretty much universal, except for those odd places that still cling to sundial- and hourglass-time and roman-numeral calendars. At midnight, on the last day of December, everywhere people kiss and hope for better or less of whatever fed or tormented them for the last 12 months. And they sing 'Auld Lang Syne'. Now, if you're handing out smacked wrists for cultural hegemony, how cruel is 'Auld Lang Syne'? What does it mean? I'm Scots, and I've no idea. What is it that old acquaintances aren't supposed to forget? But still, the whole world sings it, and for a moment the world becomes Scots. Incoherent, lachrymose, amorous, clumsy and fond. I'd never spend New Year in Scotland, either.

I suppose what I was frightened of most in not spending December at home was the loneliness. The deep sadness of the uncoupled. The longing of the expatriate. But I never have. I'm fonder of the old island when I'm away from it. The irritations and the embarrassment are ironed away by distance.

I think the best Christmas was in Bali. We roasted a suckling pig and in the middle of the hot night, jumped into the swimming pool. And instantly it began to rain: curtains of steaming tropical rain. A gift from home, a little touch of festive England.

A sense of loss

Smell is powerfully evocative but sadly we've become a planet of nasal wimps. From Asian fish markets to black Africa, now's the time to follow your nose.

Paris used to smell of bakers, pissoirs, pastis and dark tobacco. It was as alluring and decadent a scent as a city could wear. It was a nasal, atonal clarion; all the right notes – greed, taste, appetite, abandon, sex, philosophy and decay. If they made scented candles out of the air de Paris 1968, I'd burn them. It's the tobacco that was the unique addition. Lots of places have got piss-and-booze, but nowhere else has that absolutely distinctive smell of French cigarettes. You'd get off the train at the Gare du Nord and walk through the station and there it would be, snaking through the concourse. Eddies of it would catch the back of your throat; one of the most alluring and evocative smells ever invented, like wood and burnt nuts and spice, a sweet-sour smell. Just gorgeous.

I smoked for 30 years, and for most of them I smoked untipped Gitanes or Gauloises or froggies. Smoking them was like inhaling bottlebrushes, but the smell never stopped being nasal foreplay. Clothes and hair that smell of old blonde Marlboro are disgusting. The smell of morning-after Gitanes is a pheromone, an aphrodisiac that makes you want to nuzzle. Every subliminal-wannabe-implied-sophisticated lie that the advertising industry tried to roll into a fag paper was actually true about froggies. They really were the essence of existentialism and beatniks and tousled beds and the four-o'clock philosophy that ends in tears and kisses. It was the smell of a shrug and the atmosphere of the greatest street-side catwalk in the world.

I couch all this in the past tense because the last factory making dark tobacco cigarettes in France has just closed down. This isn't just the end of an era, it's the end of a whole slice of human possibility, a whole gossamer tear of existence wiped away. It's an extinction that's to be mourned far more than some sweaty rainforest, frightening oversized cat or wrinkly big pig with a horn in its nose. The death of froggies is heartbreaking, and I'm responsible. I used to do it and now I don't. I stopped French-kissing French fags and I don't care how that sounds.

All the smells of old Paris have gone now. No one drinks pastis, the bakeries are all out-of-town conglomerates, the pissoirs went years ago. And it's not just Paris that smells of bland-city. All over the world, the urban scent has been wiped off the olfactory map. Nothing smells of anything anymore. It's not just bad smells, but all smells. Restaurants don't smell of food. Look at the extractor fans in a modern kitchen: they look like the warp drive of the Starship *Enterprise*. We are beginning to associate natural random free-floating scent with dirt and disease and an uncontrolled atmosphere. It's the control and manipulation of our environment that's eradicating a whole sense; for us, perhaps, the most important sense, certainly our most vulnerable one.

Our sense of smell, which is closely aligned to taste, is lodged in the oldest bit of our brains. It's older than language, older than opposable thumbs. It's older than standing on two feet. It's the bit of our head we share with the dinosaurs. Consequently, smell is the most evocative of our senses. It can spring surges of déjà vu on us, resurrect affairs and Christmases past, and make dead people rise again. Smell is as close as we can get to living on our instincts. It makes you feel without an intervening thought. And we're rubbing them all out as fast as we can, and replacing them with a sort of man-made easy-smell compilation odour.

We cover ourselves with chemical imitations of safe musk and plastic flowers, the air is filled with the toilet-wipe scent of pine and lemon and the childish reassurance of cinnamon and cedar. We have had a whole invisible environment stripped away and polluted with the smell of the suburbs. This is most serious with food. Smell has become less and less an element of taste. There are things that Western children now believe have no natural odour at all: milk, eggs, chicken, potatoes, carrots, beef. They don't trust the real smell of citrus or strawberries, cheese, mushrooms; they prefer the chemically processed ones. The world can be split into all sorts of halves, haves and have-nots. But here is a new source of division: smell. And we in the rich half are the ones who are the have-nots. A fifth of our physical world is being atomised. We are becoming nasal wimps. All new or strong smells seem bad or unpleasant. We've forgotten how to be adventurous and brave with our noses; we no longer follow them. Smell is now the most striking difference between them and us.

I think you should start getting your hooter into shape. You should factor smell into your travel plans. You should seek out freshness and decay, the ancient and the freshly laid. Here are four grand smells everyone should get up

their noses before they die: a North African souk; an
Asian fish market at dawn; durian fruit; an Ethiopian
church. The best and most evocative of all smells is of
black Africa. Sweat, goat fat, charcoal smoke and red dust.
It's the finest smell in the world: take a deep breath,
jump in.

New New York

The skyline is more or less the same, but the mean streets are no longer mean. They're just irritable. And a bit dull. But you've still gotta love the Big Apple.

Previously I wrote about the singular fascination of islands and the odd micro-cultures they cultivate. I made a list of the sea-surrounded specks that I particularly liked, but I had the nagging sense I'd missed somewhere, that one of my islands had gone missing. And then, as is the nature of these things, it crashed into me in the middle of the night. Of course. The most cussedly singular of all the self-defining islands is Manhattan. Barely an island at all, cut off by only a mere moat, spanned by great girder bridges, just semi-detached enough for an odd individuality, New York, New York. The only other city apart from Edinburgh and London that I've ever lived in.

For one amazingly happy and self-destructive year, it was my city and I was its citizen. Manhattan is the 19th-century model of how all cities were supposed to look. It was a robber baron's vision of the future. But nothing dates as fast as predictions and futurology. They fix a look that is forever the moment they were conceived in. By the time I got to live there in the '70s, New York had developed the famous look of a stalled archaic thudding grandeur. The emphatic gestures of the skyline were contradicted

by the angry filth of the streets. New York was acned
with graffiti and rubbish, the roads were potholed and
riven with seeping oil and infernal steam. New York was
murky. The mafia ran utilities, City Hall was partisan and
biddable and the police were notoriously open-handed. It
was the time of the great corruption, when Nixon was being
dragged, inch by inch, down the long road to impeachment.
The stink and guilt and loss of Vietnam hung in the air
and, most devastating and depressing of all, disco was at
its most noisomely idiotic. The city had gone from being
a vision of the future to being a dire dystopian warning.
Delegations from European cities gingerly came to see
what lay ahead for them – and if they could avoid it.

New York was the urban jungle, a cautionary tale, and
New Yorkers rather revelled in their Grimm retelling of
it. They talked endlessly and viciously about murder, the
more random and salacious the better. Old ladies pushed
under subway trains for kicks, joggers gang-raped and
brain-damaged in Central Park, junkies found rotting
in the basements of Fifth Avenue apartments. New York
invented mugging. The word became a constant refrain,
the morning complaint like the weather in London or the
traffic in Tokyo. Mugging was New York's weather, New
York's traffic. So we all learned to carry nothing, no watch,
no ostentatious coat or briefcase, no smart handbag,
definitely no jewellery. Everyone walked in the same
slumped, determined, aggressive, un-eyecatching way. We
all looked the same, millionaires and muggers, students,
panhandlers and plutocrats. The midtown socialite and her
maid were indistinguishable. New York the über-capitalist
city became New York the communist one.

It invented the apocryphal story. New York was a great
omnibus of things that had happened to a friend of a

cousin of a brother-in-law of a girl at work. The rumours
were the morbid pleasure of decay. The favourite was the
one about the city worker who bumps into a tough-looking
Puerto Rican in the street. Immediately, as all New
Yorkers do, he checks for his wallet. It's gone. This one
time he's reached the end of his tether, so he turns and,
throwing caution to the wind, confronts the thief. Give me
the wallet, he shouts. The mugger, shocked at being finally
confronted, hands it over. The businessman gets home,
and there's his wallet on the bedside table.

The defining film of the moment was *Death Wish*. At
night I walked a dog in the park where Charles Bronson
meted out summary justice to street thugs. In fact, the
park was mostly populated by ancient middle-European
men playing floodlit chess. I worked as a janitor's assistant
in a Harlem school. My boss was a big Jamaican who
carried a revolver in his overalls. I was never frightened
in Harlem or on the subway I took there, but I did like the
sense of tension, the watchfulness, the worldliness of the
naked streets where wits were what you needed. I was in
my twenties. I looked like a young punk. I didn't know
any better.

Last week I read a short paragraph in the paper: the
citizens of Harlem are signing a petition to stop Columbia
University from expanding. In the '70s, Columbia was an
island of middle-class aspiration and white liberal hope
in the black and Puerto Rican underprivileged sprawl of
crime and violence. Harlem was the wicked wood where
all the bad people waited before creeping through Central
Park to rape and pillage Jews. Harlem was a worldwide
byword for robbery, squalor and racial discrimination.
Columbia, on the other hand, was secure. Well, apparently
we were misinformed. Columbia is now the problem,

and Harlem should be protected as a site of cultural and historical significance. The university is an interloper, a conglomerate whose expansion will spoil the atmosphere of the neighbourhood. And that is the final, irrefutable proof that New York, the New York I lived in, no longer exists.

The skyline is more or less the same, but the mean streets are no longer mean. They're just irritable. New Yorkers got what they fervently prayed for: law, order and garbage collection. They got a property boom and a safe island. In terms of murder and robbery, Manhattan is now one of the safest places in the West to live. It's also one of the dullest. More concerned with aspiration and appearances than life, the city that never slept now doesn't go out much past 9.30pm as it has to get into the office by 6am. It runs on the spot to CNN, not dances in the dark to Madonna. It just shows you should be careful what you ask for.

I still love the city, though. I go back regularly, walk the old streets. And like all places you return to, it's a mixture of here-and-now and then-and-there. There's a particular bright sunlight you only get in New York, and the buildings look particularly fine and defined against it, as if they're super-hyper-real. It always makes me happy, because it reminds me of being happy.

Manhattan is now a rich middle-class island with bankers' concerns and shopkeepers' worries. It has succeeded in buying off the murderers and muggers, and with them the artists and writers, the social parasites, the lounge lizards, the remittance men and the unforgiving women, the amusing failures and all those who came to the city from all over America and the world to claim social, artistic and sensual asylum from the broad bigotry of small towns and wide suburbs. They've all gone now, and they've taken the thing that the real-estate sellers, the arbitrage traders and the hedge-fund topiarists all wanted to find here in the first place. New York has once again become a prophecy of the future, a different cautionary tale about the consequences of fear: judicious tedium.

Plane miserable

It's time to empty your pockets, remove your shoes and submit to the naked x-ray in a ritual that assuages the fear of flying.

Airports come high on the list of our most dreaded environments, somewhere after the paedophile wing, crematoriums and the Korean Football Association. We really don't like airports. They manage to be both incomprehensibly technocratic and redneck tacky. They are relentlessly efficient and infuriatingly slow. Aeroplanes rarely crash when you consider the impossibility of flight; it's just the sheer absurd act of contrived faith that we believe that if you drive a jumbo jet at 160 miles an hour it will suddenly become lighter than air, and have enough lift to hoick 400 fat atheists who have all lied about their cabin baggage across a continent. Airports are particularly annoying because they don't do what it says on the box. On the box it says 'Welcome to Mother Teresa'. Well, it does if you land in Tirana, Albania, which is, to my knowledge, the only airport named after someone who thought you'd be better off dead. At least in Italy you can be welcomed to Leonardo da Vinci, a man who at least thought flight was probable.

Airports imply freedom and effortless transportation. You go to sleep in Europe; you wake up in Latin America. But first you have to go through a quarter-mile of queues that are like taking part in the Middle Ages. The queues

part and re-form and split and become free agents and
then they reconstitute themselves again, constantly
disintegrating, re-forming and moving. It helps if you
think of an airport as being a Petri dish incubating some
world bacillus. (It helps, but I'm not sure what with.)

Airports are all bisected: they are problem and solution,
frustration and freedom, departures and arrivals. They
are the yin and yang of travel, the oldest, most ancient
fear and relief. One of the things that differentiates *Homo
sapiens* from our ape cousins is the ability to track ahead,
to see a destination before you get there, to assume a route
to it. The trepidation of leaving the cave and the fire, and
then the relief of getting back, are implicit in airports.
Our emotions in them are not entirely post-modern fury
at the human speed of things or the pre-digital confusion.
Airports are one of the very few areas of life that haven't
naturally evolved into being better, easier and more
comfortable with time, technology and experience. We
now look at the advertisements for flying in the '40s –
with their subtle mix of military can-do and ocean-liner
obsequiousness – with envy. It was supposed to feel like a
suave and sophisticated thing to do, this flying lark, with
bone china and beds with real sheets. The airport was a
comfortable, covetable waiting room.

Anyone who has travelled through a hub airport in
America recently will know quite how miserable an
experience they have managed to make it. There is now
the added humiliation of the naked x-ray. American
passengers are beginning to rebel, to refuse to be
intimately examined in these infuriating, run-down cattle
sheds. This is the most health-and-safety conscious nation
in the world, where people will sue over hot coffee, where
they print warnings and disclaimers on both chewing gum

and assault rifles, and the combined demands of home security and health-and-safety have piled misery onto the dumb rote tedium of security lines. The one things that's worse than being asked to remove your shoes, open your laptop, take off your belt, empty your pockets and remove your watch is to have to stand behind someone who has to do all these things and seems to have a magician's number of pockets all of which contain small change, keys, phones and a half-full hip flask. Security trumps every other requirement or desire. Security is a ratchet that turns relentlessly to move every conceivable, statistical, minute chance of human interference and aerodynamics. The security consultants and the pat-down officers and the monitor-watchers and the conveyor-belt facilitators aren't going anywhere, and they really don't care if you are. The acquiescence to the innate goodness of airport security has become an absolute that no one in an airport is even allowed to question. The faintest mention of terror or box cutters will get you arrested and draconian charges dumped on your head. We all understand why this happens and, though irritated, we abide because we accept that safety is ultimate and we know why we go through this.

But actually, flying is safer than almost every other form of getting around. You are in far more danger on the streets of most cities from fundamentalists or international terrorists. It's just that the consequence of a bomb or a fanatic on a plane is so catastrophic – but then no more so than a bomb on a train or a ship. Most 13-year-old boys could work out five or six scenarios for urban Armageddon that are worse than blowing up a plane. Hollywood spends a great deal of money thinking of them, and we live with that. We understand all the possibilities and we compare them to our ordinary coming and going and we reckon up

the odds and we think they are so distant, have so many
noughts, that we just forget about it. Wildebeest can't
insure against lions, but they understand that statistically
it's unlikely to be them. But this natural, rational
discounting of possible danger against this necessity of
continued living becomes a whole new equation in an
airport. The odds are perceived to be far more perilous,
the chances far steeper. It's as if someone had blocked off
half the holes on the roulette wheel.

I have a feeling that this is a realisation, a projection,
of the innate and constant fear of flying itself. We perceive
the danger to be added on to the already dangerous, nay
impossible, activity of flying. It isn't natural, it shouldn't
work. We may understand the dynamics of a wing passing
through the resistance of the air, but still it's a meagre
trust to hand your life over to. We rationally understand
that flying is safer than riding a bike or even a donkey,
but emotionally we know it's some unnatural alchemy. We
accept the absurd level of insurance security because it is
somehow a manifestation of a votive ritual that assuages
our nervy fear. If you comply with the demands of security,
if you put your moisturiser and toothpaste in a plastic
bag, if you carry no sharp objects (not even a threatening
necklace), if you turn off your mobile devices, then you
will assuage the god of levitation who will gently deposit
you in this thin and fragile cigar tube safely in Tenerife.

We call them airports and not airfields or dromes
anymore after the very first one, which was in
Southampton. And that really was an airport. It was
where the flying boats landed, like the one in Sydney
Harbour. Southampton Airport was also where the Spitfire
was first tested. Its designer, R J Mitchell, was a driven
man. He designed 24 aeroplanes between 1920 and 1936.

He died in his forties of cancer. It was said he worked himself to death. He said, 'If anybody tells you anything about an aeroplane which is so bloody complicated you can't understand it, take it from me, it's balls.' And that could be the motto of all airports.

When the RAF took the design for his fast fighter he was informed they were going to call it the Spitfire and he replied that it was just the sort of bloody silly name they would choose. He personally called it the Shrew. On such insignificant footnotes do the destinies of nations turn. Imagine the Battle of Britain fought by Shrews. The few Shrews to whom so much was owed.

A-grade Belgrade

With more than its fair share of troubles in its past, Belgrade might be one of Europe's gruffer cities, but it's also a place of striking beauty.

A Frenchman, an Italian and a Serb all end up in hell. The Frenchman begs to make one last call home to see how his family is coping. The devil says fine, it'll cost you an extra thousand years in the flames. The Frenchman agrees, and tearfully listens to his wife shagging his brother. The Italian begs to call home to see how his daughters are doing. That'll be an extra thousand years in the flaming pit, says the devil. So be it, says the Italian, and weeps as he listens to his children selling the farm. Now I want to call home, says the Serb, and grabs the receiver. He hears his neighbours robbing his house. How much is that, he asks the devil, who replies that it costs nothing. How dare you, shouts the Serb, you took a thousand agonising years off the frog and the eye-tie, what's wrong? My pain not good enough for you? No, no, says the devil, local calls are free.

I don't really do jokes, and neither do the Serbs. This one, which I suspect is an international pizza-topping joke, was told to me by a Serb with not so much a straight face as a rigidly palsied one. He told it to me in a monotone without embellishment to prove that Serbs had a sense of humour, that they could be as ticklish and ribald, as warmly hilarious and avuncularly clubbable as any other damn nation in the world. And not only that, but it also proved that Serbs were secure and sophisticated enough to tell jokes at their own expense. Though, he added, the sentiment that Serbia was semidetached from hell was only to be used in a ribald setting and under no circumstances should be exercised as an assertion in a non-humorous context, as that would be likely to get your kidneys removed the secret way.

And that's quite enough about Serbian jokes. Let's just leave it at the inarguable fact that Serbs have a fine, sharp, well-honed, pointy sense of humour, but they choose not to use it unless provoked. And if they do, you'll most likely be laughing on the other side of your face. So if I suggested you spend your next European holiday in Serbia you'd probably say that I was joking. Pull the other one, you'd say. Shall we go there after the health spas of Moldova and the restaurants of Kyrgyzstan or before the beaches of Cardiff and the bracing fresh air of Athens?

There's no getting around the fact that Serbia has a bad reputation. It's always had a bad reputation. Obviously it's been brushing it up in recent years just in case we forgot why we were avoiding it in the first place. I've just been, and admittedly I went because it was on the way to somewhere else. I was travelling up the Danube trying to get to Budapest and there was Serbia in the way. But, I have to tell you, it's a pretty fabulous place. A surprisingly fabulous place. Mostly what I mean is Belgrade. It's beautiful. Impressively grand. A 19th-century place built out of vanity and pride, which are two of the best emotions to build on. Modesty and self-deprecation may be admirable in people, but they're an anticlimax in urban planning.

To begin with, it's on a river, and as anyone who's been to more than three cities will tell you, the propinquity of large bodies of water is a prerequisite for a really first-rate burg. Belgrade is on the confluence of two of them. It also has a castle. A very impressive castle from multiple centuries with many impressive walls, keeps, turrets, et cetera. A river and a castle are the makings of a flush in the city department. Belgrade is also a city that likes to do its living outside. There are cobbled streets packed with cafés whose tables join up into long, winding promenades of flirtation and vicious argument. With Serbs, it's often difficult to tell the difference.

There's one street of cool bars that's known as Silicone Valley because of the quality of the breasts on display. When I say 'cool' it is in a particularly Slavic way. It is a particularly Slavic cool – that is to say cool in the way a Chinese Elvis look-alike contest is cool. Serbs don't really do Western cool. What they do is posing in a manner that implies there might be some cool going around. This is the only place in the world where I've seen an adultish man wearing a T-shirt that says 'Amateur Porn Star', and if you think that's a total absence of cool, then I have to tell you that he had his girlfriend with him. How chic do you think she felt?

I see you've been staring at our women, my joke-telling guide said. No, no, go ahead, Serbian women are famous for being the most beautiful women in the whole world. A discussion on which nation has the most beautiful women in the whole world could collapse the United Nations. All I can say is that Serbia would be unlucky not to find itself in the quarter-finals. Serbian women are very striking: lanky and heavy-chested, long straight hair, generally of some kitchen blondeness, high cheeks, wide eyes, strong features set in expressions of man-killing disdain. I never saw a Serbian woman smile. Not once.

I mentioned this to my hilarious guide. No, they don't have a sense of humour, he said. Oh, so your sense of humour is solely a male, masculine thing? Yes, he said, it's not nice for women to laugh. Would you like your woman to laugh? Maybe she'd laugh at you. Yes, I can see that would be difficult.

I really did love Belgrade, and I wanted to love the Serbs. They are a nation on probation, and have been for a hundred years. They suffer from being squeezed between larger, gaudier, richer neighbours, the Ottomans and the Habsburgs. Serbs dreamt of a greater Serbia, and they got Yugoslavia instead. They desperately want to be relaxed and laid-back and turn up at the party correctly dressed. But they can't leave the history thing alone.

There is some fantastic food here. I ate brilliant slow-cooked buried lamb, one of the best dishes of mixed offal I've had for years and marvellous Serbian coffee with doughnuts and a sort of yoghurt cheese sour-cream thing. (Serbian coffee is really Turkish coffee, but without the punch in the throat for calling it Turkish.)

Really, you should go to Belgrade. You know, my guide told me, we are the only city in Europe that's been bombed four times in the 20th century. Oh yes. Once in the First World War by Austrians, twice in the Second World War by Germans, and then Russians, and last and not least by NATO. Well, fancy that.

Urban maul

Of all the slums in the world, none is beneath hope or beyond care and optimism. Except those aesthetic and intellectual shanties that money buys.

Last year, somewhere on a street that probably doesn't have a name at a door without a number on the outskirts of a hot, dirty city in a suburb that's been called something collective and unlikely, a tired man with a fearful family finally put down his meagre but heavy enough collection of plastic bags and worn buckets and sticks and tarpaulins, sunk to an earth floor, looked at a tin roof and said, we're home. His wife would've sent a child to get some water while she lit a fire. They weren't to know this, this frail, delicate family, but they were a tipping point. As they stepped over this particular threshold, they marked an astonishing and memorable moment in the march of mankind. They will never know it, and we will never know who they were; all we do know is that somewhere, out there, someone moved into some city and turned the world urban.

For the first time in all of history, indeed in all the history of all the species that came before our species, more humans live in the city than in the country. We are now more metropolitan than rural, and that has taken 10,000-odd years to come about. From the first settled agrarian communities in the fertile crescent between the Tigris and the Euphrates till now, there has been a steady drift towards pavement and brick. We are civic hominids, collective folk. We may not like or trust each other's company. We may need to make elaborate rules and etiquettes just to hang out together, but it does seem to be our preferred habitat. We are street-corner creatures rather than the denizens of hedge and copse.

The most common address in the world, the place you're most likely to find most of us, is a slum. I'm fascinated by slums. I'm fascinated mostly because I don't have to live in one. Very few people visit slums. I've only ever come across two cities where they do tourist trips to their slums: Rio and Johannesburg. In Rio, you can go to a favela on a safari in a Land Rover driven by a guide dressed up like Sanders of the River in an African white hunter's hat. You're told to keep your hands inside the vehicle and not to antagonise the wildlife; if confronted, don't make any sudden moves. The favelas in Rio are integral parts of the city. They climb up hills and have famously the best views.

All slums are places that exist outside of control, without regulation or plan. They are amateur and desperate and extreme. They have an energy and an ingenuity that is inspiring and depressing. Like the 'flying toilets' of Kibera. Kibera is a huge slum outside Nairobi, possibly the biggest in Africa. There is precious little water and absolutely no sanitation for one million people, so they defecate into the thin ubiquitous plastic bags of Africa and then fling them with abandon, possibly with joy, into ditches, onto roofs, at passers-by. The bags collect in great stinking heaps and wait for the rains to wash them into the water table, through people's bedrooms and kitchens and across the slimy roads.

Slums are always temporary. No one moves into one or builds one and thinks, this is me, this is forever, this is Dunroamin. But they remain, calloused and crumbling, always evolving, growing like human aviaries. Slums are at once disheartening and a terrible indictment, an accusation, but they are also a marvel, a hope, an ambition. And they have the intrinsic beauty, the majesty even, of the human will. Like the packing-case-and-plastic shanties that crawl up the motorways and roundabouts and the corners of Bombay, a city that is such a magnet to the subcontinent that it's considering locking itself away behind a wall like a vast gated community, insisting on invitations to get in. It is a great economic nightclub.

My top six slums are: the Mercato, the rambling warren of a market in Addis Ababa, where khat is sold. The shantytowns of Antananarivo, the capital of Madagascar, that look quaintly like huts in Dutch paintings, in this, one of Africa's most beautiful cities. Glasgow East: tough and gritty, an ancient enclave of hardened arteries and attitudes, but with an indomitable grim humour. The Afghan refugee camps in Peshawar: this was the most beguiling and is now possibly the most hideously dangerous city in the North-West Frontier Province. Kaliningrad, a Russian enclave on the Baltic between Lithuania and Poland: utterly forgotten, once a closed military city, now a festering pocket of organised crime, pollution and decay. And by far and away the worst slum in the entire world, the City of the Sun in Port-au-Prince, sprawling along the shore, bisected by sluggish rivers of sewerage, this great shadow Hades of greed, black magic and fear is the most mesmerising place I've ever been. A silent set-aside of depravation and terror where, conversely, I met some of the kindest and warmest people in all of the West Indies. The City of the Sun is the bottom of the bottom of the pile, the end beneath which it is difficult to fall. But still here you see children carrying satchels going to school, nurses in uniform going to comfort richer sick people, workmen carrying bags of tools to make nicer cities more habitable.

Nowhere is beneath hope, beyond care and optimism or do-it-yourself miracles. Except the slums that money buys. I'm writing this in New York, and New Yorkers spend a lot of time complaining about the gentrification of Manhattan. The city has grown monstrously expensive; money has seeped into every poor corner and knocked it through and exposed its brickwork and put renewable hardwood floors over it. Money has bought order and quiet and civic responsibility and health and safety and an early bed. It's improved the coffee and the sushi, but it's also driven out the things people move to cities to get. The enthusiasm, the naughtiness, the young, the pretty, the unpublished poets, the unhung painters.

All cities move up and down an organic scale, from the flying toilet to the dog-walkers. All cities are making a slow progress from bottom-rung to we've-arrived. There is a point in the middle where they are for a moment, for a decade, so marvellous a cosmopolitan mix of grit and ambition, of anger and laughter. Of all the slums I've been to, the two very, very worst, by a long street, were Monte Carlo and Las Vegas. Nothing is as filthy and dispiriting as the places money made for its own edification and greed. Aesthetic and intellectual shanties, moral flying shit-bags.

Reality bites

If you want an authentic travel experience, try Albania: there's something very liberating about visiting a country with nothing going for it.

We don't travel to see places. We travel to see things in places. For instance, I've lived in London all of my ambulatory life and in that time I've never once been to St Paul's Cathedral, and neither have I seen the changing of the guard, and I haven't had tea at The Ritz. They're just not part of my city. But for many people passing through, they are the city.

I've always wondered how many natives of Bangkok have had soapy four-hand stress-relief massages, such a central feature of the sophisticated executive visitor's visit. When I asked a masseur, she said almost every bloody man in Bangkok was up for a bit of stress management, including her worthless, good-for-nothing husband. I should say that I am the only round-eye man I know who has been through Bangkok and not had a massage. Frankly, I get performance anxiety on my own. So the point is, I have a strangely inauthentic memory of Bangkok.

Never trust or travel with someone who says that they can show you the real somewhere or take you to the city that the locals know. If you'd been visiting London last week and seen my local city, you'd have read the papers for an hour, then sat in a doctor's waiting room for half an hour, got a prescription, gone to the chemist, waited another half an hour, walked for 10 minutes, then retraced your steps back to the chemist's because you'd forgotten the razor blades, and then you'd have gone to the supermarket and bought four bananas. You'd have eaten a banana in the street, then walked home to watch an old John Wayne film all afternoon. See, it's authentic, but it's not any more real than going to the Tower of London, Madame Tussaud's, eating jellied eels, sinking 10 pints of warm brown bitter and doing the Lambeth Walk.

Nobody has secret access to a real country, as if the rest of the country was unreal. I was thinking about this because I just got back from a place without any places in it at all, Albania. Its only memorable monuments are Roman, and no one's ever going to come up to you at a party when you get back and say, with an imperious drawl, did you manage to see the temple or the church or the palace or the museum? I wish you'd told me you were going, I could've given you a few tips and some addresses.

The problem with Albania is that it's way too real. There are no unreal bits to retreat into. The moment you step off the plane at Mother Teresa airport, it slaps you with the cold fish of reality: the place is a mess. It's not just a mess, it's a punch-drunk mess. The wonder of this Adriatic sliver of the Balkans is that it's still standing. It has gone 12 rounds with every political and economic system known to hominids and a couple of them that are exclusively its own, and it has lost on points to all of them. Communist, fascist, warlord, monarchist, you name it, Albanians have been beaten senseless by it. Punchy, but still game – that's Albania.

And there is something very relaxing about going to a country that has absolutely nothing to recommend it. Normally, you travel and you get a list that's longer than a Chinese menu of places that you simply have to see, and you spend your time committing cultural triage in churches and palaces and feeling rushed and guilty and oppressed by the piles of cultural beauty. Well, there's no danger of that in Tirana.

No, there's nothing to see, and there's nowhere to be. There's not even anything to eat. This is the only country I've been to that doesn't have a national dish. Or even a disgusting local delicacy that you have to take home with you in a tin with a picture of a smiling peasant girl hugging a cow on it, or a cardboard box that leaks nameless fat from whatever preserved body part it holds.

Tirana has nothing to commend it at all. There is a fetid canal, of which the main claim to your attention is that it used to be worse, and a big out-of-town supermarket where they search your bags on the way in, presumably to stop you leaving confusing and subversive stuff on the shelves. The countryside has even less in it than the city. It's just big, deserted, green and mostly perpendicular. The seaside is the Adriatic, which isn't really a sea at all, more a non-tidal warm brown effluent soup that slops between Albania, Italy and Croatia.

It is all a blessed relief from the obligations of being a responsible traveller. You can properly live like a native: that is, not do anything at all or go anywhere. Anything you choose to do, by its very nature, is authentically local, because there is no tourist thing to do. At all. I met a public relations official for the tourist board. What do you do all day, I asked. Well, he said, like everyone else, I sit in cafés and deal in foreign currency and speak to my brother in Milan and get him to send me designer sunglasses. But what do you do about tourists? What tourists, he asks, suddenly worried and looking over his shoulder. No, not real tourists, pretend, future tourists – the ones you're supposed to be attracting. What would you tell them. Oh, I tell them we are the land of unspoilt possibilities. Well, that's true except for the unspoilt bit. It's more a land of spoilt possibilities.

And then I tell them we're going to be the next Croatia.

You'll be beating them off with a shitty stick.

You're just saying that, aren't you?

I'm afraid I just am.

Although I enjoyed Albania almost more than I can say, I feel bad that I haven't recommended a single thing. There should be at least one attraction to make tourists feel guilty for missing and that, in turn, you can superciliously ask a returning businessman if they saw. So this is it, the must-see ... It's Tirana's natural history museum. It's easy to miss, because it looks like a condemned building. Indeed, in any other European country, it would be a condemned building. But walk in, and don't mind that there's no one else there. There's never anyone else there. Just two floors of the worst stuffed animals in the world. Gimpy gannets, lopsided goats, fish that look like sausages, a bear that has the face of a hairy Quasimodo. Rooms full of nameless bleached things in urine-yellow bottles. And boxes with pinned flies inside cases full of random dead flies. I have never been to a national gallery that is such a perfect and poetic metaphor for the country it lives in. It is perhaps the greatest national museum in the world. You simply have to see it. Just remember to turn the lights out when you leave.

The last word in travel

Living to tell the tale (and telling it well) is almost as important as the trip.

I have a thing about thesauruses (thesauri?). I can't be bothered with them; won't have one in the room I write in. I know it's a snobbery and a stuffiness that seems to go along with 'I'd rather be lost than ask for directions' and refusing to have luggage on wheels. It's not the words I mind. I've got at least a dozen dictionaries, and I'm staring at four serried shelves of reference books. I've got books of quotations, books of slang, etymology, classical allusion, classical history, biblical concordances, opera, film, national biography and the birth of South Africa, but I just won't have a thesaurus. It's a question of propriety.

You can only travel as far as you can describe. I'll put that the other way around: you can travel to the extreme edge of your vocabulary – after that, you might as well not bother going. There is certainly little point in coming back. The inability to describe what you've seen and done is a chronic, terminal intellectual disability. You know how overwrought adolescents say, I couldn't love anyone who couldn't love *The Outsider* or late Picasso or Nirvana, and you always say, oh for God's sake, get over yourself? Well, I realise I hold something similar. I couldn't love someone who couldn't tell me where they'd been, what they'd done and what they loved in a compelling manner.

I once met an explorer, not an adventure tourist – a real heart-in-the-mouth, mapless, first-foot explorer. He'd been up mountain passes in the Tien Shan that had never been mapped, strung between mountains that had no name. In the company of the most remote and introverted people on the globe, he'd walked on his own with a yak and a small mute boy for a month.

He'd been kidnapped, escaped, arrested, shot at. He'd had a bit of a time. And when I asked him what it was like, he said: cold. Cold and? Wet. Cold and wet. And had he come back from the roof of the world with any insights? Yes. Pack a spare pair of shoelaces. Broken laces were a constant worry, apparently. And that was it. He took a sort of taciturn pride in the unspoken journey, locked away like a schoolgirl's diary in his head. And I thought, that place is still unknown. The untrodden paths and the nameless peaks are still anonymous. Your experience was a waste of breath. And shoelaces.

On the other hand, I once found myself with nothing much to do but wait in a village in northern Uganda. Uganda's a peerlessly beautiful country, its burnt red earth a bright undercoat colour that dusts everything with a rusty orange. I sat at the side of the road with a 13-year-old boy who couldn't go to school because his mother was ill and he had to help her. I asked him to tell me about the three-mile journey he made to get to the schoolroom. He made it an exciting odyssey, a high adventure. Each step had moment and significance. This was where he'd seen the eagle pick up the kid. This was where his grandfather had fallen off his bike. There was the best mango tree, but you had to fight the monkeys for them. On and on, I was utterly engrossed, his singsong reedy voice drawing form over the colours. It was the only journey he'd ever

made from his village. And the next day, I had to drive
to his school in an NGO's Landcruiser. The journey took
20 minutes, and it was just another road in Africa, but I
watched it like a movie.

The lesson is, if you want to increase your vocabulary,
don't read more, get out and look harder and farther. And
that's the reason I don't like thesauruses. They sell you
other people's words. They're not yours. The language isn't
the verbal evocation of your experience, it's some ten-
bob adjective which is what you think will decorate your
experience more elegantly. The words you choose need to be
really yours. Ones that travelled with you. The vocabulary
that saw what you saw and saw what you did, not some
smart-talking PR you hire later to tart up the experience.

Words are important. They don't have to be posh or
rare, they just have to be honestly come by. I think I can
always tell thesaurus writing. It has a spongy overstuffed
pout, a slippery, out-of-sync fuzziness. Sentences that
obscure rather than illuminate. The test is to speak them
out loud. If it doesn't sound like a plausible statement, it's
thesaurus writing.

I know it's a bit late to introduce a subject, a theme
to this column, but I was asked to write about luxury,
and that's what made me think about the thesaurus,
because luxury is a word I almost can't bring myself to
use without inward mockery. And here we come to the
problem with the language. Generally, if you have a
breakdown while manoeuvring English, it's your own fault.
And it's because you're mistreating the finest mouthful of
expressions ever invented. If you can't say it in English,
you can be pretty sure you can't say it at all. But there
are some things you can say, but you wouldn't want to.
Like luxury. And luxurious. Luxuriant. And, nastiest of

all, luxuriate. For all its subtle, muscular chiaroscuro, English is particularly duff at figuratism. The descriptive terms for effortless, thoughtless supine enjoyment are all embarrassing, to say or to write. They make every sentence sound like the brochure for a health farm.

I enjoy a pleasurable experience as much as the next man. There's nothing wrong with being rubbed, scrubbed and grubbed into a pinkly gleaming state verging on insensibility, if that's your cup of single-estate first-flush orange pekoe. It's the word that sticks in my craw. Luxury, for me, has associations with tastelessness, snobbery, waste, boredom, blandness and insincerity. It rarely arrives on its own, usually travelling with the help of 'timeless' or 'effortless'. On a dirty weekend, luxury can usually be found luxuriating with sophistication, creating the glacially botoxed thrill of sophisticated luxury, an expression which is inevitably attached to two-inch wider, three-degree more acute airline seats.

Luxury, and its braying, swilling, posing and poncing mates, lives in the half of the world I travel to avoid. (The trips to St Tropez and the Caribbean being merely part of my gruelling working life, that is.) Of course, having written all that, I had to go and get a thesaurus just to see who luxury sleeps with. Here is the unadorned list, and I think it's rather profound. I still won't use one, but it's given me a little more respect for the old lexicon.

Maybe there is a beat of irony behind all the synonyms. Read this as a poem: *convenience, comfort, cosiness, snugness, creature comforts, luxury, luxuries, superfluity, lap of luxury, wealth, feather bed, bed of down, bed of roses, velvet, cushion, pillow, softness, peace, quiet, rest, repose, quiet dreams, sleep, painlessness, euthanasia.*

Dawn of a new era

Post-apartheid, Johannesburg has become the luckiest place in the unluckiest continent.

A tokoloshe is a Zulu demon, a nightstalker, a sprite goblin. Familiar, it lives under your bed and comes to you in the dark. South Africans put their beds on bricks, on tins, wrap spells around them to prevent the tokoloshe climbing up.

What he'll do to you, if he does, is never mentioned. It's too horrible. The tokoloshe isn't some cosy fairytale because of naughtiness to add a frisson to bedtime, he's a real five-star terror. And what makes him different from every other night-sweat apparition, what makes every tokoloshe unique, is that he's singular. Each of us invents our own. He is the creation of our deepest, most horrific fears – a bespoke, made-to-measure personal demon.

So when you wake in the stillness and you can hear the faint scratching of hard fingers on the headboard and the sharp-toothed muttering, you know it's coming just for you. It isn't interested in anyone else. The tokoloshe can't be bought off with lies or flattery. You can't trick him. He knows you outside in.

The tokoloshe is a particularly brilliant and terrible invention, a horror version of psychoanalysis – the psychoses, irrational fear, the weakness that is inside all of us manifest as homunculus. It's also particularly apposite to South Africa.

Ten years after Mandela and de Klerk, truth and
reconciliation and elections, South Africans are still
soggy with disbelief that they've managed to avoid a civil
war. The longer they go on with majority rules, the more
astonished they are that it still works. They've become
immensely forgiving of occasional outbursts of irrational
fury or bad behaviour because, 'Oh, it could all have been
so much worse,' they shake their heads and sigh. For
10 years, they've got away with it and there's no obvious
rhyme or reason. Africa is the very last place you'd bet
on having a mass agreement of contrition and forgiveness.
And South Africa is the only country in the world to
uninvent a nuclear bomb.

Of course, everybody gained. It was a platonic triumph.
One up for humane civilisation. But – and it's a huge but
– in practical terms most people are, if not worse off, not
doing much better. Unemployment could probably beat
employment in a fight. And for the first time, this is as
bad for young whites as blacks. Affirmative action has
reduced their options. The finance minister is running a
very Thatcherite strict economy which thrills men in suits
in New York and London but is testing the long view of the
townships. And then there's AIDS and illegal immigration
from every other country in Africa. There's a strong
export-stifling rand and a drought. It's tough all round
but – and this is an equally big but – it's also ridiculously
hopeful. South Africans smile and look at the sky and say
'Pinch me, am I dreaming, did we get away with it?'

The last time I was in Jo'burg six or seven years ago,
it was a frightening city, unravelling into medieval crime.
People who had stuff lived behind barbed wire and
spikes with multiple dogs and alarms and private security
firms. They drove like fighter pilots sealed in 4WDs with

snub-nosed .38s on their laps. Their kids were taught to run in zigzags and lock themselves in their bedrooms and put their fingers in their ears. They all still cooked braais in the garden, played tennis, got drunk, but the strain was terrible. You could see it in their eyes – the wear and tear of terror. Jo'burg rode its luck until it almost died of nervous exhaustion. Everyone knew someone who'd been, well, never mind, we don't talk about it. The centre of the city emptied and died, the suburbs became mid-western shopping fortresses.

But now, this time, I got out of the airport and was amazed – it's a new place, really astonishing. Areas you'd never have walked through have grown cafés and boutiques. There's an atmosphere. It feels like a collective decision to get better, to get on and up. There's still miles of razor wire, you've still got to watch yourself, but Soweto's a tourist destination. You can get a tour, eat lunch, buy a wire motorcycle souvenir. There's arts and music – loads of music. There's theatre and there's the new apartheid museum which just rams a lump down your throat. As a rule, I don't like walking round museums that have been twisted into social engineering. There are lessons to be learnt from the past and the past can be accessed through things, but the reason for putting things in museums shouldn't be to make kids polite citizens because, in general, it makes for self-righteous exhibits and the kids smoke behind the bookshop and swear at passers-by. But this one is something else. There are very few artefacts, it's a journey through history commissioning an execution of apartheid, told with photographs and film and hundreds of televisions. If that sounds dull, then it's because I'm not explaining it properly. It's a cross between a moving scrapbook and an art installation. It's

also the most thoughtful and emotional couple of hours
I've spent in a museum for years. The divisive story is told
inclusively and if you've never been to South Africa, you
can have no idea how difficult, restrained and courageous
that is. The museum is a lesson in how history doesn't
have to have consequences or at least not the ones that
were written on the packet. Fate is open to apologies.
Classes of black schoolchildren milled round me as ever
in Africa, neat and beautifully turned out, in exuberant
uniforms. A year ago, I'd never have suggested to a tourist
that they take time to visit Jo'burg but now you've simply
got to. Not just the apartheid museum and the townships
and the markets and cafés, the music and jacarandas,
and the high, dry veldt, but you should go because this
is the luckiest place in the unluckiest continent. This
year, the UN pointed out that Africa tipped from being an
agrarian continent to an urban one. More Africans live
in cities than in the country. And almost all tourists who
come to Africa with the best liberal intentions come to see
animals and wilderness – very few come to see Africans.
No pride of lions is as exciting as an African market, to
walk through an African street is more entertaining and
enthralling and a lot more inclusively hands-on than a
drive in a game park. If you want to feel the rhythm of the
dark heart, then go to an African city. I'd go to Jo'burg.

Personally, I think it was the tokoloshe that made
South Africa hold back, divert the consequences of the
past. South Africans lay awake in the hot night and heard
the panting and the muffled sharpening of little goblin
pangas and knew what the fears made flesh would bring.
The tokoloshe still lurks under the bed, but the longer this
normalcy goes on, the smaller the fears that feed him.

A roach by any other name

Cockroaches live everywhere we do, but they aren't our competitors or the scuttling, creepy enemy to be squashed underfoot. Rather, they are fellow travellers.

Who was Gregor Samsa, and what does he have in common with nuclear Armageddon, the Rwandan genocide and an Australian rugby league team? We'll come back to that.

A couple of years ago I wrote a story about goldmining in Johannesburg. The shaft goes down two kilometres. The alleys come off the central shaft like the veins and arteries of a body, and a new capillary is blown out every morning and the rubble cleared every afternoon. At this depth, the rock is almost too hot to touch. When it was formed, when it last saw the light of day, the sky was red and there was no atmosphere. It's pre-oxygen. This rock is older than life. In the seam of rubble, with the mile or so of roof held up by crooked steel jacks, in the light of my helmet, I was seeing something that no one and nothing had ever seen before.

I crouched in the heat and the dust in this little rock cellar thinking deep, deep, deep thoughts. And then something tickled my hand – I looked down and there was a cockroach. Three hours before, this was solid, hot, mineral blackness, and here was this bug, questing, pushing the frontiers of cockiness. Roaches live everywhere we do. In the hot, stony dark they were here eating the residue of the explosives.

'Cockroach' is, of course, the answer to what Gregor Samsa was. He is the subject of Franz Kafka's *Metamorphosis*, the guy who wakes up to find he is a cockroach. Roaches were always supposed to be the main benefactors of a nuclear war. Cockroaches are what the Hutus called the Tutsis in Rwanda, making it easier to slaughter them. And I'm told it's also the New South Wales rugby league side's informal nickname, for reasons I didn't ask or wish to be told. As far as I'm concerned, you can never know too little about sport.

But the roach's nuclear radioactive invincibility is now being questioned. In universities in the '70s, no discussion of the Cold War could finish without someone pointing out that as cockroaches were able to sustain more than six times the radiation of humans, they would become in a flash the top of the rearranged evolutionary pyramid – and would quite literally inherit the earth and all the wreckage thereof, ushering in a new age where six legs and two antennae were good.

Not so, it turns out. We were wrong about nuclear annihilation and the Cold War, and we were also wrong about the cockroaches. They can indeed endure more radiation than us (radiation particularly afflicts cells that divide. Ours tend to divide quite a lot; roaches' only divide when they're changing out of their work clothes, which is about once a week). But scientists are now saying the critters would last only a year or two after we'd gone. They would pine away without us. Cockroaches, it transpires sweetly, aren't our competitors or the scuttling, creepy enemy to be squashed underfoot. Rather they are our fellow travellers. We're joined together at an alimentary level. We feed them, and without us and our refuse, they would waste away.

This has made me feel quite differently about the roach, and I have had what can only be called a Gregor Samsa moment. I am searching for my inner cockroach. I must strive if not to love them, then to realise we share the same bathroom and kitchen in life for a reason. I must understand they are as much allegorical as insect.

'Cockroach' was a term some radical Latin American writers used to identify the invisible, persecuted immigrant workers in the United States. They even had a song, 'La Cucaracha'. And I'm trying to remember memorable or entertaining cockroaches that have passed though my life. It's difficult.

There was the kitchen in Delhi where I went one night to get a glass of water from the old colonial stone filter and thought the floor crunchy with spilt sugar, until the next morning when I saw my footprints perfectly captured in hundreds of dead roaches. And there was the London hotel restaurant where I was briefly a dishwasher. If you flicked on the light in the scullery, the room seemed to shiver – there was a momentary flicker, like a camera shutter. It was the carpet of roaches sprinting for cover. I also remember a vast one I reluctantly shared a shower with in Port-au-Prince, and the 500 I shared a boiled terrapin with in Saigon.

I'm trying to find some fondness, some liberal sense of multicultural, multi-species togetherness with the cockroach, but I can't. Likewise, I suppose I'm also trying to find something positive and winning to say about parties. It's a Freudian slip, that asked to contribute to the magazine's party issue I come up with insect vermin. But

I've always been very bad at parties. Even in the short, frenetic period when I was good at them, I was really appalling at parties.

I have been to some astonishing ones over the years. Just taking New Year's Eve, for example, there was a candlelit castle which sat in the sea off Sri Lanka where we had to wade up to our waists in the warmly lapping Indian Ocean to get to the turbaned waiters with the champagne. There was a swimming pool in Bali in a thunderstorm with a roast pig. A tented camp in the Kalahari with a dozen Germans in fancy dress. A yacht in the Caribbean on a sea fluorescent with DayGlo. There have been penthouses and snowy cabins, with punch and mulled wine, with fireworks and cabarets, with cocktails and topless samba dancers. With people I've loved and people whose language I don't speak. And every time I've yearned for the first bellow of 'should auld acquaintance be forgot' because I can't wait to forget all of them. To get through the sticky alcoholic kisses and the soggy bear-hugs so I can leave and go home to bed.

I have never been to a party I didn't think could be improved by fewer people. The only thing I enjoy less than other people's lavish hospitality is my own. Years ago I gave up giving communally. It made me too miserable. I clearly haven't come to terms with my inner cockroach, the ability to be singular in company, to catch a common mood and gain happiness from the propinquity of happy people. A jolly community depresses me. Small talk is too much of a mouthful. I'm bad at flirting and worse at being flirted at, and I despise myself for not being able to just join in, to get up and dance on a table once in a while.

Oh, to be Gregor Samsa, to wake up one New Year's Day to discover that at last, finally, I'd metamorphosed.

True believers

Utah may be better known for the fervour of its resident Mormons, but this state is also home to the West's most pervasive morality play.

Give them the barest, skinniest streak of half a chancy idea, and people will believe anything. Somewhere, sometime, someone has put their hands on their hearts and believed everything. There is no human thought so logically bankrupt that someone isn't hanging it up as one of the solemn truths of their lives, and God gave us Utah just to prove it.

Utah is pretty much monopoly Mormon. Now I don't want to wee on anyone's cherished and precious soft centre, but the history and beliefs of the Mormons would make a Rastafarian blow his cheeks out, roll his eyes and click his fingers in incredulous wonder. But then I quite admire that. Faith is all about a step into the mystical. It is the trust in the unknowable. So the more unbelievable and unknowable, the bigger the leap of faith. And when you come from the land of Anglicanism, which is no more than dipping your toe in while holding on to the secular handrail, I'm rather envious of the belly-flop belief in Utah.

Utah came to me as a revelation, which is biblically appropriate. I didn't mean to visit it – I was actually in Colorado for a kid's holiday, but we just sort of edged on in to Utah, and it's astonishing. Outside of America, it's not in the top 20 states people want to visit. In fact, the Mormons only settled there after they'd been moved on from everywhere else with pickaxe handles. There is the story that Brigham Young promised that after their 40 days in the wilderness he would lead the Mormons to the land of milk and honey that God had promised them. The weather got worse and worse, and the land got harder and harder, and the Indians ever more hostile and the Mormons were complaining and moaning, and finally they came across this great lake. Here we are, said Young, this land will bloom with our crops and our livestock; this is the land of milk and honey. And he took a drink of the water. And it was salty. Okay, newsflash, he spluttered. God says you can have as many wives as you can handle.

Utah is a breathtaking landscape of red sandstone bluffs and weirdly sculptured cliffs and precipitously balanced stone. It has pinnacles and canyons and deserts and huge mountains all arranged in a shimmering beauty. The desert is full of aromatic plants that smell of turpentine and stunted acid pine and juniper. In the evening, it's like opening the door to an old garden shed. We stood on 2000-foot cliffs and looked down at rivers that had carved serpentine canyons. In the sunset, the whole pink and russet sky cast a last glare over 100 miles of wilderness that in scale and colour and texture, and surreal imagination, is unrivalled anywhere. It all ended up with the horizon of Monument Valley.

And there were so few people here. This was a place that made the Lake District look like a cottage garden, and the South of France a municipal roundabout. We camped on a high cliff and watched the world without a single electric light or human noise. It was as Brigham Young first saw it, except without the maniac voices in my head. Above us the vapour-trails of jets flew smart people from Los Angeles to New York, and I stared at them as they turned pink and then headed into the clear dome of the night sky. They were as distant and as alien to this place as you can imagine.

All landscapes come with an atmosphere, a sense of narrative, a back-catalogue of plot. They aren't created with it; we bring it with us. It's our contribution to the picnic of nature: we give it a reason. It doesn't want one or need one, but we do. We have to organise the view into some sort of coherent story that has some place for us. We geomorphise the world to fit it into our heads. The thing about Utah is that while it's astonishingly conceived and echoingly empty, it has a whole library of plots. This landscape of Utah is the theatre for the greatest genre in the world ever. This is the set and the background for cowboys.

There is a continuous sense of déjà vu here. You know this place, you know what happens. You have the soundtrack in your head. It's very nearly a spiritual experience. The cowboy story has gone around the world. This landscape is the Vatican of that story. It is riding into the sunset. It is the church of a man doing what a man's gotta do. This landscape is the great tablet of rock that the commandments of good and evil, and righteous endings are written on.

We all know the code of the West, the strict morality of the cowboy story. For 100 years, it's been the simile and metaphor for our behaviour. It's one of the guiding clichés of politics, and the model for conflict. And it's all here in these silent, massive, tortured soft rocks. This is the truth about Utah's arid land. But it isn't The Truth. This place is also home to the enigmatic predecessors of the Indians who were such a necessary part of the cowboy story. They themselves are relatively recent immigrants. Before them in this place lived pastoralists who were simply called the basket people. They grew minute corn and squash and wove baskets. Apparently they cooked in baskets. They had failed to learn pottery. Now missing pottery is pretty basic. Not getting the wheel or writing or condoms is understandable, but not discovering mud is frankly, in evolutionary terms, an F.

Nobody knows why the basket people failed to notice clay. Perhaps they looked up at the astonishing landscape and thought, better not touch the dust children of the big stones. You know people will believe absolutely anything. You look at this panorama and believe cowboys and Indians and getting the girl and riding off into the sunset.

Spice of life

Temper your fears and love Calcutta.

India is the way station between tourist and traveller. You remember the declension: I am a traveller, he is a tourist, they are trippers. Well, New York's a trip, Bali's tourism, Varanasi's travelling. I must say that I think the well-rounded and inquisitive life includes a bit of all three, but there are people who never get to travel. It's not money or opportunity – it's cheaper to be a traveller than a tripper – they're too busy or too squeamish or too frightened.

And India is where they stumble. Not travelling to Turkestan or Texas is understandable. They're ugly, angry and the food's filthy, the accommodation grim. Of course, there are wonderful things to see and experience, but it's like eating whelks – only the really keen see the effort worth the reward. But India has the lot. It's the destination of destinations. Whatever it is you're looking for, India has it with six arms on.

But still people will shy at it. 'India? I don't think I could. No, I know it's wonderful, but the poverty, the begging, the deformity, the lavatories, the smell.' And I've come to realise that no amount of proselytising will change their minds; best to put away the snaps and say, well, it'll still be there if you change your mind.

Having said that, I want to try to get some of you to go to the most exciting and rewarding place I went to last year. Even those travellers who happily embark on

India will be unlikely to have taken the detour to take
in Calcutta. Those on a limited budget, or pressed for
time, will find other places come beckoning more sweetly.
Calcutta's reputation is not good. In fact, it's probably
the all-round bookies' favourite for the worst place in
the world. The black hole of black holes. Mother Teresa
could've gone anywhere in the world in her bid for
sainthood, but this was the mother lode.

Now, I'm not going to lie to you, Calcutta is probably
the most polluted place there is, and though the UN
no longer keeps a league table because it's pejorative,
mention Calcutta off the record and they'll hold their
noses and make throat-slitting signs. A large proportion
of flights have to divert because visibility is so bad.
There are 11,000 factories, 750,000 cars, all on 24km of
collapsing road, and the millions of inhabitants all cook
on charcoal, so a yellow pall hangs over the city, giving it
a rather romantic and mysterious gloom. The 90 per cent
humidity makes the air thick; it tastes as if you're sucking
coke. Blow your nose at the end of the day and it looks as
if you've been nasally attacked by a sturgeon.

And it's communist. One of the last red governments in
the world, it can barely get a collectivised game of bridge
going. They banned computers because they thought
they'd put people out of work. While other Indian cities
leapt ahead riding the software boom, Calcutta was left
with its smoke, draconian capitalist tax, no investment and
high unemployment.

The reason you should book a ticket right now is
because this is one of the most entertaining and beguiling
places you can see that no one you know who doesn't wear
a wimple has ever been to. Because let's face it, part of the
pleasure of travelling, as opposed to tourism, is exclusivity

and rarity. The fact is that Calcutta has the lowest crime rate of any comparable city in India. You'll find more beggars in Alice Springs. Thanks to the communists, there are no more power cuts, and because of compulsory schooling, there is a high literacy rate.

But that's not it. Calcutta is the heart and soul of India's post-Mogul culture. Tagore and Satyajit Ray are from here. This is where Indian drama, poetry and novels are gestated. It boasts an embarrassment of world-class universities, medical schools and specialist colleges. Just walk down College Street and see the biggest open-air bookshop in the world. Thousands of stalls with piles of second-hand books. Whatever you want, from a tome of obscure jurisprudence to the plays of J.M. Barrie, they're here. And up a flight of stairs next to a bookshop is the coffee house once called the Albert Hall.

It is the Brasserie Lipp, the Spago of Calcutta. A beautifully run-down, sparse room where turbaned waiters serve coffee and mutton curry on tables rubbed smooth by millions of elbows. This is where Bengalis come to argue. There is a table of theatricals; here, newspaper editors; and over there, a gaggle of girls gossiping. The thing that Bengalis do better and more than anything else is argue. They are the past masters, born with opinions and rhetorical flourishes. The rest of India says a Bengali would rather talk than work.

Calcutta was invented by the English on the banks of the Hooghly, the last stretch of the Ganges. It was a stupid place to build a city, but that never stopped the English. And it became, for most of imperial history, the capital of an India that ran from Burma to Ceylon. I initially came to look at the crumbling architecture, that glorious propagandist style, part-Mogul, part-Roman, with a touch

of Home Counties vicarage. It's impressive, and a guided
walk around the old capital, its churches and graveyards
with their sad inscriptions putting a brave face on the
vicissitudes of rebellious natives, turgid bugs, rotting
alcohol and broken spirits, is all fine, but if you come
from a post-colonial country, this will all be familiar stuff,
though not on this scale.

What you should do is sit on a *gadh*, a landing stage
on the river, and watch the astonishing life. Or go to the
flower market and watch them make garlands. You might
go to the Kalighat temple and see the most striking votive
statue of Calcutta's patron goddess. Go to the new market
– you should eat Bengali fish with mustard in banana
leaves, and Calcutta's famous puddings and sweets. You
should play cricket on the *maidan* in any one of the
deathly serious games. And you should start an argument
with a local.

I loved Calcutta because it's a city on the way down.
Cities on the way up are all very well, but they're also vain
and aggressive. Cities that have been something and seen
stuff have stories to tell. Places can be trippers or tourists
or, like Calcutta, they can be travellers.

Flight of fancy

- -

*You don't have to travel far
when you're taking a holiday
from reality. Simply put a new
spin on history, buckle up and
enjoy the ride.*

Have you ever taken a holiday at home? I don't mean
stayed at home instead of going on holiday, done a bit of
mending and decorating instead of flirting and fornicating,
but actually pretended to be a tourist in your own town.
It's a bizarre experience. It first came to me when a friend
asked if I would look after a couple of his friends who
were passing through London for five hours. I took the
nice people to dinner and then asked them what they'd
like to do with the three hours that were left.

We've never been to London before, she said. We'd like
you to show us everything. Everything? I doubt if we'll
ever come back again, he added, with a tinge of pride.
We got in the car, and I said, I'll see if we can cover the
whole city. It might be a bit tight, but we should manage
it. Let's start here. On your left is the site of the Battle
of Waterloo (Hyde Park). Next to it is the famous Battle
of Hastings (Kensington Gardens) where Harold got the
arrow in the eye, and down there is the beginning of the
Channel Tunnel.

Where does Charles Dickens live?, asked the husband.
Funny you should ask that, we're just passing his house

here – Albert Hall. It's big because he lives here with
the cast of most of his books. Except Miss Haversham, of
course. She lives down the road in the V&A Museum. We
saw the Thames, where the Spanish Armada was defeated,
and Harrods, where Henry VIII bought all his beds. You can
find The Blitz on the fifth floor, along with Cockney spirit.

After a couple of hours of driving around a very
small patch of Kensington and Knightsbridge, the happy
couple had seen all of London. And I don't think it's any
exaggeration to say they'd experienced most of London's
gay pageant and a great deal of English history as well.
Here was the bench where Richard Curtis first met
Thackeray. This was where Keira Knightley fell in love
with Mr Darcy. That newsagent is where Sweeney Todd
bought his copy of *Coarse Fishing*. Don't look, but the man
running it now is the illegitimate son of David Niven and
Enid Blyton. That's the traffic island where Charles I was
executed by Mussolini, and here's where Bonny Prince
Charlie bravely but foolishly danced a highland fling on
a zebra crossing before taking the equally bonny boat to
Skye, which is just next door to Battersea Power Station.

Stop, stop, said the chap. I can't take any more. How
can you live with so much history? It's all over you,
everywhere, everywhere you turn, coming out of the
windows and through the cracks in the pavement. There's
a story and an anniversary in every bump and brick – how
can you bear it? Back home, nothing's ever happened, or
nothing that would count as history.

Oh, I just think it's so exciting, said his wife. But I
couldn't live with all that stuff happening under my feet.
So exhausting. We like a quiet life. Yes, the quiet life, he
added for emphasis. There's nothing like the down-home
feeling of boredom. Mind you, we wouldn't have missed

this trip for the world. We'll be talking about it for, well, I expect for as long as we have teeth. It was a nice thought.

Hemingway pointed out that Paris is a moveable feast. That wherever you went in the world, as Bogart had it, you always had Paris. Well, I think that history is like that. The past should be a moveable picnic. You can use it to brighten up a dull town or a tedious suburb. Why shouldn't the Battle of Lepanto have taken place in your municipal boating lake? And Marco Polo would've stopped at your out-of-town shopping centre if he'd had the time. Attaching the past to specific lumps of geography is very narrow-minded and pedantic. The past happens in books, films and photographs and in your head. You can take them where you fancy.

I realised the great relative truth of facts released from geography the second time I went on safari in Africa. The first time I went, I asked the questions everyone who's confronted by Africa asks. Mostly, what's that, and, why's it doing that? I must've asked it a couple of thousand times a day for a week. And on each occasion I was given a sturdy answer, until I was weighed down with stout and hard-wearing facts. When I went back the second time, I started with the whats and the whys again. I realised almost immediately that I was getting completely different answers. The go-away bird was actually a grey lory and not a Gabriel's banded cross-beaked hoebird. The lion doesn't roar at a decibel-level that will kill a junior wildebeest with the vibrations of terror. That acacia isn't known as Hottentot birth control because the seed pods can be used as condoms. I realised that my first guide had been making up things as he went along, and I, far from being angry or feeling a fool or being cheated, liked him all the more for it.

I had been shown a tailor-made, bespoke place. Anyone can learn stuff from books or experience. But to take the trouble to invent a place specifically for my pleasure was very touching. And, still, a lot of what we know about the world is what people who are keen to please us have told us. History and geography and the factual past are a relatively recent invention. Before there was real biological and topographical Africa, there was a continent of ghosts and ancestors, of myths and fables. The bushmen will still tell you, with a certainty that will cold-cock a polygraph, that the moon is one of mister praying mantis's swollen testicles.

Before history, we had the myths of gods and heroes. We still move around the classic world saying, this is where Odysseus slept, this is where Hercules had a bit of a barney. The other world hides under the certainty of maps. When I was a child, my bedroom was Troy, and then Treasure Island and Narnia and Mowgli's cave. If you've got a day, go on holiday around your own neighbourhood. Give it a lick of relative truth. A polish with a myth.

Out of place

----

*Algiers is not your usual
Mediterranean port, but it is
memorable. Sometimes the places
that stay with you the longest are
the awkward, demanding and
frightening ones.*

'Is this your last time in Algeria?' the man in the cake
shop asked me. He obviously didn't get much of a chance
to practise his English. Foreigners are rare hereabouts;
everybody asks 'Is this your first time?' (or indeed your
last), as if wishing the rare visitor to say 'No, no, I come
here often, spend my summer holidays here, do business,
have fun,' in the hope that visitors might return like the
swifts that dogfight over this great white city. People
don't come here unless they're from here. There are
precious few journalists. Getting visas is like getting a
transplant – someone had to fly from London to Algiers
to get mine, and I'd just come here for three days to write
about food.

You forget that this is just the other side of the
Mediterranean; Spain is over there, Italy there, France
over there. This is the same pond we crowd around in the
summer, but not at this bit, not in Algeria, which has some
of the most beautiful and empty Mediterranean coastline.
Algeria is a place out of place.

Algiers is a memorable city, perhaps the most imposing on the south side of the Mediterranean, built around the bay, which is the great natural harbour that made it the port of choice for the Barbary pirates shipping kidnapped slaves from as far away as the Black Sea. It started off as Berber, then was invaded by the Arabs, then the Ottomans, and finally the French. Now it's confused and furious.

The stucco front of the French town elegantly curves in a promenade around the shore, echoing the Rue de Rivoli, looking rather like Marseilles. The windows and shutters are all painted a clear, beautiful blue. The broad boulevards are shaded by ficus trees that have been pollarded into a parasol hedge. Behind the fading and well-thumbed colonial city is the kasbah, crammed and higgledy-piggledy, a dark expressionless scatter of alleys and winds and staircases. This was the Ottoman city, the boroughs that incubated the bitter war of independence from the French. Of all the grim and desperate conflicts of colonial disentanglement, the battle for Algiers was the most bitter and tragic. In an inglorious final chapter for Western empires, this was the most shaming, and has left psychological scabs on the winners.

The volume and the intensity of the bitterness that Algerians feel towards the French is shocking. Only the very old could even remember the colonial period, but still it's an abscess in the mouths of almost all Algerians, and it informs and colours all political thought.

As always, when you come from Old Europe to the Maghreb it's astounding to see the rivers of youth that run everywhere, through every doorway, round every corner, torrents of the young. North Africa looks like the whole world's playing truant here in an open casting for an epic remake of *West Side Story*. Gangs of young boys, skinny,

sharp-elbowed, dressed in the kit of British, Spanish
and Italian football clubs, handsome and inquisitively
malevolent, stand in the wings of the city. There's precious
little for them to do but practise their walks and their
cool looks.

The unemployment figures are a state secret, but they
run pretty high. The children play-fight and shout and
sulk, and the rest of the city throbs irritably by, the traffic
grinds and hoots and waves its impotent hands. Cafés
are full of men drinking tea and animatedly shouting at
each other. Women with shopping bags barge through the
pavement with faces of implacable determination. The
whole place vibrates with a gnarly repressed anger, which
would be overwhelming for a visitor if it weren't leavened
with a broad streak of dry, acid humour.

Algerian conversation seems to be mostly threats and
insults. The threats are vicious, the insults brilliant. You
spend your time gasping, and laughing. For more than
15 years, Algeria has been impaled on one of the most
terrifying civil wars of the last century and this is barely
reported because few journalists want to take the risk. The
fight was between a military-backed residually centralist
communist government and a radical fundamental Islamic
movement that was imported by Algerians who had gone to
fight with the Mujaheddin in Afghanistan.

The terror that has stalked the streets of Algiers and
the villages of the interior is of a nightmarish intensity.
The army and the fundamentalists raised each other
in a pitiless game of revenge and monstrous example.
Until now, they've slaughtered and tortured, threatened,
blackmailed and terrified themselves into a state of
shivering inertia. It's not peace, it's a breathless, crouched
horror. People talk of the war in the hushed tones that

gothic fairytales use to describe the monsters in the night. The war is the hideous, flesh-eating, throat-slitting prayer-mumbling orc. It's not over, it's just a war that's consumed all its own oxygen and is gasping in shock.

As I write this, a busload of soldiers have been ambushed in the night. The war, the curfews, the fear, have wiped all the public fun off the face of Algiers. People talk of the night-life that once was, the sophistication of the bars and the cafés, the beauty of the women, the little pastries, the cocktails, the glamour. This was a great city with wit, poise, élan and passion. It had a Mediterranean culture, with writers and poets and musicians and sentimental torch singers crooning love and betrayal. They're all gone. There are cafés, there are restaurants, but as the sun sets the city is given over to roadblocks, and police checks, and men with judicious machine guns.

Along the coast, there are seaside resorts with bars where men go to drink and take chubby, busty girls with vicious blonde hair and faces of brazen shame. And the singers still croon their warbling yearning over Hammond organ backbeats. The drinks are ridiculously expensive. Men become ostentatious and they hand fistfuls of notes to the singers who in turn mention their names with praise. These nightclub acts become the amplified praisers and everybody else listens with the casual good humour that you would use for listening to the stewardess's safety instructions. They drink and they cheer and they blow a month's wages to hear themselves proclaimed rich, attractive and happy by a sequined lounge act. It's an act of extraordinary catharsis, both pathetic and touching.

The food here is good and simple and generous – lots and lots of sardines and mint tea. The sun warms, the breeze from the sea is welcome. But you probably won't be visiting Algiers. It's not a holiday destination. It doesn't yet offer those things that holidays demand. But it is nonetheless memorable. Sometimes the places that stay with you the longest are the awkward, demanding and frightening ones.

At twilight, before the fist of the sun fries in the sea, the golden hour bathes the white stucco and families collect on the promenade at the very edge of the city around a small fair with roundabouts and rides for toddlers and coloured lights and tinny music, clowns' faces, livid sweets and balloons. It's like the desperate carnival at the end of a bad dream. Boys play football and army conscripts shadow-box.

The holiday pitch

Another golf course and swaying palm tree. Why are countries so bad at revealing what is beguiling and unique about themselves in tourism ads?

Up here in the old hemisphere, this is the dream season, the time of reverie, of trance travel. This is when we all imagine what it would be like to be hot, to walk without rubber soles. It's the holiday tease-time, when the brochures land with the thud of a ripe mango on the carpet and TV is sultry and juicy with advertisements for countries flashing their take-me-I'm-yours sides.

I'm constantly amazed at how un-self-aware travel ads are. They are presumably made by bright men in coloured spectacles with comedy face-hair and chubby girls with sagging cleavages and champagne breath who collectively call themselves creatives and have spent a year hock-deep in the freebie trough thoroughly raping and pillaging the mini-bars of the poor developing nations they've been employed to project and sell like a willing tart in the slave market. Their creative impressions of the country will have been rigorously scrutinised by a boardroom full of suited and aspirational indigenous civil servants, keen that the world see them in their best light. So how on earth do they arrive at so many golf courses?

Egypt advertises itself with the music of an Italian –
Verdi's *Aida*. Which, while being essentially a story of
ancient pharaoh-folk, is a bit like Japan advertising itself
with the soundtrack from *The Mikado*. And to the rising
arias, there's film of someone playing golf and galloping
on a horse. If you've been to Egypt, you'll know that golf
and horses are not the lasting memories. Where is the
shot of the tourist with his head in the toilet? Where is
the man in a nightie flogging a donkey to death? Where
are the charming and ornamental military policemen, the
attendant urchins chanting 'Manchester United, jingle
bells, jingle bells, give me a dollar?' And where is the
soundtrack of omnipresent Egyptian pop music, the frantic
tinny twank of unrequited love and chicken slaughter?

Last night I saw an ad that looked like a modernist
Finland in the sun, with a lot of people dancing around
in a '70s-hippie California-esque encounter-group
sort of way. Then someone played golf, and a girl in a
bikini swam, and there was a close-up of an eye with
gold makeup. Where were we supposed to be? Where
was it that I wanted to be? Not only couldn't I tell the
country, I had no idea which continent I was supposed
to be hankering after. It turned out to be somebody's
approximation of Greece. Greece? Where was the cloud of
smog? Where was the fat bloke with hairy shoulders in the
wife-beater selling bellybutton rings and ouzo bottles in
the shape of a penis? Where were the queues of coaches
on the terrifying road up the mountain? The plastic
menus with pictures of livid puce kebabs? Where was the
inexplicable bloody theme tune from *Zorba*?

Playing beat-the-intro on tourist ads is a great indoor
sport. The American one playing here at the moment
features the titles for films with states in the title, and

invites you to visit the sets. Understandably most people would be attracted to America by what they've seen on the big screen, but it's a hostage to sequels. They don't, for instance, include *Mississippi Burning* or *Paris, Texas*, or even *Birth of a Nation*. There are far more movies that would terrify you into never wanting to go anywhere near America. *Oklahoma*, for instance: aggressive baritone cowboys line-dancing in gingham. What they don't advertise, of course, is the fact that most people aren't even invited to America. I know for a fact that they don't make a Spanish version of this commercial.

Australia's ad isn't much better. Australia is advertised with the usual golfing, galloping and carefree swimming. No sign of the flotsam of bluebottles or the miasma of flies. The tagline is 'Where the Bloody Hell Are You?' Which was supposed to sound both authentically ocker and Pom-friendly, which is obviously oxymoronic. There's an old subeditors' rule that says never write a headline that's a question: it instantly invites the wrong answer. So in reply to where the bloody hell are you, most of us think, we know where we are, where the bloody hell are you? You're 24 hours in a limb-numbing farrowing cage away, watching *Friends* and *Crocodile Dundee* on a screen made out of melted plastic bags next to a Hasidic rabbi who's memorising the Torah out loud, and an infant with a mouth the size of a great white and a bladder the size of a condom nipple, breathing the communal pint of air a thousand recycled times. Have you ever thought that flying from London to Sydney is probably as ethereally intimate as having carnal relations with every person on the plane? That's where the bloody hell you are: the other side of a group heavy-breathing cluster-frot.

Why are countries so bad at knowing what it is about themselves that charms and beguiles? Why are they so unaware of their real talents and assets, so keen to propagate the pat clichés of themselves, the postcard trite, and the vanity? The nations east of Rangoon bid for our holiday money by looking identical. Bring on the clones of salaaming women in hobbling silk, some sort of hotel foyer folk-dance that's only bearable for a couple of seconds, a beach, a high-rise, neon and moonlight. A bright market with a smiley wrinkle-faced old woman, then a beautiful hostess. And, of course, golf.

From Malaya to Indonesia, they're all the same, and imply that perhaps what holiday-makers want is not an authentic experience, but a predictable generic one. Last week I watched an ad for a beach. It was so ubiquitous it could've been anywhere on the globe between Capricorn and Cancer. It was a primary snap of 'holiday': bendy palms, white sand, pale-blue sea, and I sneered and thought, who'd fall for that? And then came the punchline. With a start, I realised I'd just got back. I still had the sand in my bag and the peeling nose. It was the Seychelles, a place with a simple, binary CV: sun and sand.

It's barely been inhabited for a geological blink. It is a country blissfully unencumbered by history, plague, natural disaster, pogrom, invasion or religious fervour. It has no man-made thing that's worth crossing a street to view. It has precious little in-your-face or up-your-nose culture. It is just a collection of the most perfect icing-sugar beaches that regularly win best beach awards. But, actually, when you're there, that all comes as a blessed, remarkable relief. There isn't even a souvenir; you'd be pressed to buy a coconut letter-rack. Still, this is a place

of subtle and profound thoughts which hiss out of the surf
and rustle in the damp broad-leaf forest.

Here are a couple of holiday facts that they won't put
in the ad: the Seychelles immigration stamp is a line
drawing of the indigenous coco de mer, the largest seed
in the world, famous for being a representation of a lady's
pudendum with a Brazilian. Therefore, the only way you
can get a picture of a lady's front-bottom officially printed
in your passport is to go to the Seychelles. You can also
get locked up for 10 years for stealing a coconut. They
are fearsomely protected; this may be the most draconian
punishment in all the world. The national dish is fruit bat
curry. If you ask, they'll say, as people always do, that
it tastes a bit like chicken. It doesn't taste remotely like
chicken. It tastes like muscly liver and has bones like
snapped darning needles, but it is exceptionally good.
The fairy terns are so numerous that islanders used to
break the eggs into oil drums and sell the yolks to house-
paint manufacturers. The Seychelles is the world's largest
exporter of sea cucumbers. And there is a golf course.

Down at heel

Avert your eyes from Puglia's poverty and corruption and it's easy to lapse into the notion of idyllic Italy.

The more you travel, the more you resent expectations. If you go on holiday once a year, then the expectation is all part of it – perhaps the biggest part of it. The planning, the shopping, the brochure worship, the web's hol-porn.

But expectation is essentially wishful preparation, either for a repeat of the experience you had last year or for one that someone else has told you about. Expectations pre-suppose and pre-design what you're going to see, but they don't pre-destine. More often than not, expectations pre-order disappointment. But still they are what the travel business is based on, all that wishful photography, the mahogany prose written in coconut oil. If you travel not to rest but to be excited, not to unwind but to be wound, if you want uncomfortable in new ways rather than comfortable in the same old ways, then expectations are like safety rails or wheelchair access. Expectations are nature trail arrows in the forest, and expectations are all factor 40.

Ideally, you want to travel in neutral, without the hindrance of preconceptions. It is the great truism of abroad that the best places are the most unexpected, and they're rarely the most pampering. But it's almost impossible to travel in a state of balanced innocence.

Sit and play geographical tennis with the person opposite you in the office. You just say a place name and they say the first thing that comes to mind. You'll be amazed at the depth of prejudice and preconception you hold for the world. It was ever thus. Herodotus started it. He populated the globe with dogfaced men, people who used their feet as sun shades, and women with breasts large enough to incubate chickens. We laugh, knowing that in fact that's only true about Armenia.

Nowhere in the world is as thickly swagged and laden with expectations, wishful thinking and preconceptions as Italy. It's difficult to know if Italy actually exists under the weight of holiday romance that is laid on top of it. In Italy only the most sensitive traveller could get bruised by the pea of reality hidden under all the mattresses of wishful thinking.

Italy is most painstakingly defined by northern Europe, and in particular by the English. The English are like Italy's plastic surgeons. Every year, thousands of them arrive wearing Panama hats and stupid lovelorn grins, and lift away the wrinkles, shove ever-larger inserts into its sagging cleavage and declare that if heaven is as good as Tuscany then God's doing okay. The adoration is pretty indiscriminate. From the ruins and empty motorways of Sicily to the industry and damp fogs of the Po Valley, the latest part, the most recent part, to be massaged with the purple prose of votive Englishmen is Puglia. It is the most fashionable place to be this summer. There is plenty of scope for virgin preconception (though that sounds like an oxymoron).

Puglia is the heel of the boot of Italy, a long, thin strip that stretches down the Adriatic coast. It is principally famous for its trulli houses, small, stone, round hovels with pointy black roofs. It looks as if Italy were once inhabited by a race of Arts and Crafts hobbits. It is rustic and hot and out of the way, unless you're an Albanian or a West African refugee, in which case it is in the way just in time.

Puglia has had the sort of history you wouldn't wish on your worst enemy, unless your worst enemies were Italian peasants. They were originally colonised by the Greeks, and then the Romans, the Normans, the Saracens, the Kingdom of the two Sicilies. Most of their landlords were absent and careless and greedy. Puglia doesn't have anything worth having except for figs and olives and some fish and a lot of time. It is a very poor place, and it has been for longer than anyone has spoken their particular variation of Italian. A unified state didn't improve much or serve them any better. It's a long way from Rome down here, and the power has slipped easily into the hard hands of a particularly relentless version of the mafia. There is endemic corruption, protection, and quite a lot of kidnapping. The local government is communist. Communists like big capital projects. They like to build things. Building things is a way to a better future. Socialism has meant making this bit of Italy very built. Being poor, they receive lots of grants from the EU and the central government, so the communists build roads and business parks and spaghetti factories and high-rise housing for Albanian refugees. Except they don't build them, of course. The mafia does the building, with substandard material and poor-quality finishing. And sometimes they don't even bother finishing at all. The hulks of central planning graft litter Puglia.

But if you're English, it doesn't matter, because you won't see any of that. When you drive to Lecce, you simply won't see the miles of stained semi-slum, or the permanent roadworks, or the boarded-up petrol stations, or the blocks of apartments strung with the faded sports clothes and nylon sheets of immigrants. You won't see any of that, because your eye is refined enough to filter it all out and bask in the marvel of the finest baroque city in southern Europe.

There is no denying that Lecce is spectacular. It's baroque, but not in the way the Romans would know baroque, or the southern Germans, or the Austrians. It's not baroque like St Paul's Cathedral. It's baroque that has been learnt by correspondence school by people who don't read too well. It is a style imposed on Puglia by its absent landlords and the fourth great power in the land: the church. Have you noticed that the poorest places have the grandest churches? It's no accident. It's far easier to get money out of the destitute than the filthy rich. The poor want to go to a better place. The rich know there isn't going to be a better place.

Puglia's baroque has a folk art vitality. It's an exclamation of lust and humour and anger and the sly revenge of peasants, because in the end the peasants always get you. They outlast money, titles, power, fear and even God. All the great buildings – the cathedrals, the churches, the palaces – vibrate with an earthy mockery. It's baroque that's been applied by teams of pâtissiers. They call Lecce the Florence of the south. It couldn't be less like Florence. Florence was built from banking and insurance and monopolies and dirty politics. Lecce rises out of oppression, comes despite the servitude.

But you don't need to worry about all that. Raise your eyes above it. Only the tasteless and the ethically bovine notice the plumbing when there's a west front to marvel

at. Practise and you'll be able to wipe out the rubbish,
the cracked concrete, the water-stained office blocks.
They just disappear. The West African immigrants selling
knock-off Ray-Bans and Prada for mafia gangs will begin
to look like colourful Othellos. The Gypsy children will
be bucolic urchins. The girls will only be beautiful bodies
pacing the middle distance. Everything can be brushed
and burnished into a classic once-a-year idyll if you sit in
the shade of a vineyard's awning and feel the cold beads
of condensation on your glass, smell the cypresses and the
verbena heavy in the air, listen to the chatter of sparrows
and the thrum of crickets, smell the tomato and the garlic
stewing in the kitchen, read a couple of lines of Henry
James and think that there is nowhere quite like Italy.
Oblivious of the truth. And in many ways you're right.
There is nowhere like Italy.

The shock factor

The nastiest culinary surprises are those encountered close to home.

'This must be the worst thing you've ever put in your mouth,' said a travelling companion as the waiter presented us with the turtle. We were in the middle of a paddy field outside Hanoi, in a restaurant that was no more than an agricultural, corrugated iron barn on a concrete floor with that ubiquitous light of Asia, neon. It specialised in what my Vietnamese guide euphemistically called 'exotic food'. What he meant was stuff fished out of mud – frogs, rats and this turtle, which is what Americans call a turtle and I call a terrapin.

They come, of course, with their own handy serving suggestion. We chose a live terrapin doing its impression of a dead terrapin in a plastic paddling pool. Why anyone wants to keep these things as a pet is beyond me. Anyway, half an hour later it's back at the table, looking remarkably unfazed. Only the waiter goes *voilà!* and lifts its lid off with all the swagger of the Tour d'Argent. After half an hour of sucking the metatarsals out of gelatinous feet and fiddling about in its incredibly rudimentary digestive system with chopsticks, I realised that turtle on the half-shell is more of an event and an anecdote than a meal.

I also had the hard-boiled fertilised duck egg. This is a 12-day-old Jemima Puddleduck abortion and, frankly, though edible, it's not an improvement on the before or the after. We were offered scentweasel, a cat-sized animal wrapped in a straightjacket of bamboo, and whose furious eyes gleamed in the neon. I declined, not because I couldn't have eaten it, but because I probably wouldn't have finished it.

All of these things weren't served for sustenance or pleasure, but as mystical medicines. Medicinal food in the Third World usually promises one of two things: boy babies, or an erection you can open a packing case with. I'm continually astonished at the number of things that are supposed to be aphrodisiacs in the Far East in societies that, leaving aside Western sexual tourism, are generally rather prim and conservative.

We left. The waiter gave me the gall and blood of the terrapin in rice spirit to take away. I gave it to my driver, a man of unsurpassed hideousness. The next day he told me he'd shared it with his 70-year-old father. Together they'd had a night of depraved Dionysian excess, he winked and leered. I strongly suspected he'd got dumpling-faced and did karaoke.

The things people always imagine will be vomit-inducing usually aren't. I've eaten white flying termites, salty ants, scorpions, jewelled beetles, locusts, armadillo in the shell, agouti, warm Masai cattle blood from a gourd rinsed in urine, and giant African frog. All of the insects were delicious. In fact, I'd stop for flying ants or jewel beetles. Armadillo was tough and metallic. The agouti, a large guinea pig, was really delicious, with a thick layer of fat. The frog was filthy, the size of a green meat pie, with devil eyes. I carried it in my pocket for a day. It made a lunge for my willy; frogs will eat anything. I've never been so pleased to see anything die. It tasted like pond slime and forgotten face-flannel.

A food critic really only needs two things in order to do his job properly: no eating disorders and the gastric morals of a hooker with a mortgage. You gotta eat everything, and mostly more than once. I actively try to keep my prejudices down to a minimum. I got over my round-eye revulsion of durian fruit. It tastes of garlic, wine gums and rotting liver. I quite look forward to it now.

I think in the First World we have the illusion of choice and sophistication, whereas in fact the range of flavours and textures we consume for pleasure is getting smaller and fewer: we're down to dumbly bold and inoffensively bland. So many things have single polite flavours; we're cutting out the complex and the strange.

In Iceland, they eat what is probably the most difficult thing I have ever had to put in my mouth: year-old buried shark. The flavour of ammonia is so strong you can taste it behind your eyeballs. And seal hand preserved in whey. In Reykjavik these are dishes of identity – they link modern Icelanders with the astonishing hardships of their past. It's edible heritage. They're also ferociously drunk when they sit down to the table.

There is the shock of the new, and then there is the shock of the familiar but hidden. The truth is that when you eat something threatening, disgusting, poisonous abroad, it's sort of straight up in your face. When they offer you dog, they don't call it low-fat, organic, hand-reared, street-smart meat, they call it dog. And you can go and see it out the back. They serve stuff with its teeth in and its fins on. A durian is a durian, and you can tell it's coming three rooms away.

But at home, food arrives by stealth. You never quite know – it's cloaked in euphemism and simile, wrapped in advertising and association. You never can be really

sure what this more-ish thing is actually made of. William
Burroughs said that the naked lunch is when each of us
realised, properly realised, what was actually on the end
of our forks. The most shudderingly disgusting thing is
food that's pretended to be your close friend, but is really
a sordid, child-molesting, gut-rotting sociopath. The naked
lunch, the vilest thing you put in your mouth, is when you
realise what mechanically recovered meat actually means.

And the worst thing? Well, the worst I ever heard of was
a friend who'd spent three months in Pakistan and craved
chocolate beyond reasoning. At the airport, she found a
stall selling Rolos. With nerveless fingers, she shoved
four into her mouth. They were fakes, frauds, copies
filled with gutter water. The glissando from expectation
to fathomless disgust in that is pretty unbeatable. But my
worst? Honestly? It was a hamburger from a caravan at an
Eminem concert. Without doubt, by a country mile, the
most disgusting thing I've ever put in my mouth.

Bohemian rhapsody

*Paris of the imagination is as
real as the city itself.*

I love Paris in the spring. Paris is where good Americans
go when they die. How are we going to keep them down on
the farm after they've seen Paree? We'll always have Paris.
No city has been anthologised, crooned at, soliloquised,
rhymed and mooned over like Paris. My favourite quote
is from Haussmann, the man who designed the place. He
said Paris was a sinister Chicago. According to my atlas
there are 10 Parises. One in Ontario, Arkansas, Idaho,
Illinois, Kentucky, Missouri, Tennessee, Texas, Kiritimati
(Christmas Island) 155 degrees north by 157.3 degrees
west in the Pacific Ocean and, of course, the one on the
bend of the Seine in the flat plain of northern France.

Paris is also a prefix for style. For coquetry, for
sweetness, elegance, it's a tease. In fact, there are far
more than 10 Parises. Everybody who has ever been there
carries Paris away in their head. It glitters in reverie. And,
more than anywhere else in the world, Paris is also a place
that lives in the minds of the people who've never seen it,
a capital of the imagination, an international virtual city
where finally we can all let go and perhaps be the person
our present circumstances won't allow. You could write
that book in Paris, paint that screen, screw the tatin off
the tart. You could wear velvet and wave your hands. You
could sit in a café all afternoon. You could get drunk for
breakfast. Paris is the get-out-of-responsibility-and-guilt

Never Never Land for the put-upon, the buttoned-up and the guiltily diligent and obliged.

No place in the world, with the possible exception of Hiroshima, has had such a comprehensive PR makeover as Paris, because it really wasn't always like this. Before the French Revolution, Paris was famous for being filthy, dark, smelly, dangerous and pestilential. The medieval city huddled over its own disgusting mire, while its denizens slit each others' throats and poxed whores passed on syphilis, widely known as the French disease. Paris was where you ended up if you were too deranged, feckless, dangerous or too disgusting to be allowed anywhere else.

The revolution changed everything. What was a proper murderous horror show of random terror to live through was seen as a beacon of reason and hope in places where you could sleep peacefully at night. It is ever thus with liberals. The revolution became trendy. Everyone wanted one and, of course, no one actually wanted to go live in Paris. So the sort of people who did move in were artists, writers, misfits and ne'er-do-wells, and they in turn grew to be romantic, just as long as you didn't have to live next to or eat opposite them. Revolution had been so successful for Paris it just kept on having them all through the 19th century, becoming more and more romantic and ideal as more and more people got shot, locked up and died of cholera.

The artists and writers got better at being ne'er-do-wells, who in the end did well, and the city got a makeover. Haussmann, the chap who thought it was a sinister Chicago, redesigned the city into the grid of reason, an ordered duty. That is the familiar map of today. It's actually an open prison. It wasn't done through order and

beauty in long walks thinking lofty thoughts. It was done
so that they could put down the annual revolution quickly
and efficiently – the boulevards are for moving troops,
the wide vistas are fields of fire, the great roundabouts
artillery positions. Paris was the only modern city
specifically designed to facilitate the economical massacre
of its own citizens. Who says the French have no sense
of humour?

I first went to Paris in 1969, six months after the last
abortive revolution when the students, Peugeot factory
workers and couturiers' zip stitchers had taken to the
streets and the theatres. And de Gaulle had lost his nerve
and gone to check on the loyalty of the Foreign Legion
in Marseilles. It's so typically French that every other
revolutionary in the world takes over power and the radio
station, but in Paris they storm the theatres. Six months
later when the car workers and seamstresses and the
police had all gone home, the students were still there
on stage having 24-hour philosophy-athons and passing
motions of solidarity with the anti-aircraft gunners of
Hanoi. The paving stones were still ripped up and there
were piles of loose cobbles at the side of the streets on
the Left Bank. Gangs of CRS (Compagnies Républicaines
de Sécurité) riot police lurked in malevolent huddles
sucking on gitanes. Paris still had public pissoires
and existentialists in cafés. I remember seeing Jean-
Paul Sartre in the Deux Magots. I'm not sure this isn't
communist editing of memory but I do certainly remember
it. At the age of 16, Paris hit me with a sucker punch:
Sartre and beautiful women with boyish haircuts carrying
poodles, policemen in capes, booksellers on the Seine,
Courbet and Gèricault in the galleries. I'd just read *The
Outsider* and *Down and Out in Paris and London* and I

was a pushover for Paris and have remained hopelessly
besotted ever since.

What actually did it for me was breakfast. My father
had installed us in a pension in the Rue St André des Arts.
Every room looked as if it had been decorated by Colette
and cleaned by Edith Piaf. Breakfast in the morning
was a baguette with butter and jam and milky coffee.
Unexceptional, just like breakfast at home. Except that it
was utterly exceptional. The bread had an eggshell crust
and a soft white centre that smelled of comfort. It wasn't
the white steamed ready-sliced stuff of home. The butter
was as pale as death and had a creamy sweetness that was
a thousand tastebuds from the sputum-yellow over-salted
Anchor stuff I was used to. The jam was thin and formed
pools in the butter and tasted intensely of strawberries, not
the thick, livid red anonymous fruit of England. The coffee
came in pottery bowls and tasted of that particular French
combination: hot, with milk and chicory. The apparent
familiarity was what made the reality so astonishing. If the
French had eaten herons' tongues and can-can dancers'
sequins for breakfast, I would have been excited but not
shocked. I realised that all my life I'd been eating a pale,
sad shadow and that the food in England was a horrid
charade compared to this. This was perhaps the most
important breakfast of my life. It was the beginning of a
lifelong fascination and adoration for food.

It also taught me that the things that surprise you
and move you are most often those that are closest to the
familiar. And that Paris's great trick was quality. It did
the same as everyone else – it just did it in silk and by
hand. It was a city that had invented proletarian revolt,
yet made its living out of exclusivity – from frocks to soup
to whores.

The Paris I saw in 1969 was already disappearing and when I go now it's almost completely vanished. The cobbles are gone and the pissoires. The art's all been moved and Les Halles – where I ate onion soup at five in the morning with a restorative eau-de-vie and at lunchtime a dish of chicken stewed with crayfish – has been taken over by pizza, cappuccinos and public mimes.

But there is enough Paris in my head to shroud the reality with a purple existentialism until I die. I will continue to see what I want to, which has always been another of Paris's great tricks. She was an ugly old dame who convinced everyone she was really a beautiful young ingénue. She smelled of sewers and sweat and we sniffed pastis and violets. She talked ineffable bollocks and we heard charming romance.

Paris is a confidence trick that was invented in the 19th and early 20th century by a collective act of wishful thinking. An act of auto-hypnotism made by writers, artists, musicians, poets and plain girls in good hats, who levitated the city to be a demi-utopia of brilliance, an arty afternoon humping. Paris was and still is not exactly a lie, but a fantasy, and very little of it has anything to do with the Parisians, who, despite history, culture and cuisine have managed to remain an earth-bound grasping, bad-tempered lot of scowling les misérables. As Hemingway said, Paris is a moveable feast: you take it with you as a picnic in your head. And it's a city that's often best visited from the comfort of your own home.

The end of the world

----

*An island of serenity and awe,
Iceland is experiencing its
economic woes as a footnote in a
history shaped by contrary forces.*

Iceland is a singular place, stuck up there, halfway
between Europe and a fairytale. A patch of land that
wasn't there in a geological yesterday. It's still hot from
the oven, bubbling and spitting, lavarous and sulphurous
with the fumes of Hades. It has vast glaciers and winter
winds that could flay your face, but also ponds that could
boil you alive. It's bathed in green Nordic light and eggy
gas and is one of the most contrarily rewarding places
on earth.

It was only discovered almost a thousand-and-a-half
years ago by a lost Viking, and when the first settlers
landed in 870, they set up their ridge-poles for their halls,
which they had to bring with them, because there weren't
any trees. They found, in the rocks, a couple of Irish
monks already there. Hermits, who had made what must
be one of the most hopeless and hopeful journeys ever, at
least until Laika, the Soviet cosmodog.

The Dark Age monks set out in coracles, which are
simply buckets made of woven twigs and tarred leather,
without maps, trusting only in God, searching for
solitude. They travelled up the Hebrides, past Orkney
and Shetland, already into some of the most dreadful and
difficult seas in the world, then on to the Faroes and, from

there, into nothing. A frozen, grey, howling nothing. These were people who believed the earth was flat and the sea full of monsters, but they believed in God more, and either His guiding hand or the most blessed luck brought them to Iceland.

Without wood to build or burn, without any land animals to eat or dress in, just fish and seals and puffins, they had found the mother lode of solitude. If you're in the awe business – and we must assume that monks are – then this is the Tiffany of awe. The Ringlings' four-ring circus of awe. There is enough solitary awe in Iceland to keep a mildly righteous fellow struck dumb for a lifetime. But just to show that God also has a raw and wry sense of humour (or perhaps it was just the damnable luck of the Irish, who can't resist a punchline), having got through this one-way journey of unsurpassable dread, and finally having found this beatific, chilly loneliness of eternal meditation, a package tour of heathen Vikings turns up and, you've got to admit, that's funny. It is the coldest and wettest shaggy dog story in all of the Dark Ages.

From here, Leif Ericson discovered America. The Icelanders invented the first real parliament in Europe, the Althing. And then, after a millennium of hardship and hysterical subjugation by first the Norwegians and then the Danes, they fished for cod and whales and husbanded sheep and rode horses the size of kelpies, drank like plugholes, ate sheep's heads smoked over their own dried excrement, wrote epic poetry, played chess, knitted, believed in fairies and grew to be the most enlightened and liberal people in the world.

What we're talking about here is an island bigger than Portugal, larger than Hungary, but with a population about the same size as Wollongong, Australia. Iceland,

the most unpromising piece of new development in the
northern hemisphere, has produced a mythic combination
of characteristics that are the most enviable oxymoron
available to people: poet fishermen. They have also given
the world three Miss Worlds and a Nobel Laureate in
literature. Plus Björk and Sigur Rós. And no army. And
that's not bad for a country where it's dark half the year
and that would lose a fight with Canberra.

Iceland also managed to amass a per capita income
that made it the richest country on the planet. It did this
by ... well, actually, no one's quite sure how they did
it, but the Iceland bubble makes the Dutch tulip mania
seem reasonable and subprime mortgages positively
cautious. And then it all went puffin-shaped. The island
went from being one of the richest countries to falling
back into the Dark Ages, without an intervening period
of Enlightenment. The fall wasn't precipitous, it defied
quantum physics.

All of which is why I went back. What does a country
look like, what does a country feel like, when it can't
afford a banana? No, really, they can't afford a banana.
Exotic fruit are off the menu. And seeing as there are no
trees here and the mean winter temperature is below zero,
anything that doesn't grow on a seal is an exotic fruit.

I don't know what I expected, which is rather what the
Icelanders feel; they don't know what to expect, either.
But they do expect that it will be cold and wet and tough,
which is what life is supposed to be like if you're an
Icelander. This brief interlude where, for a season, the
country became an Ireland of the north, is deeply un-
Nordic. They are facing a future without kiwifruit, without
Mexican beer, without the updates for *Guitar Hero* and
the box set of *30 Rock*. They're facing it with a phlegmatic

thirst. They are drinking and reciting poetry and singing, in dirge-like choirs, the old songs, and riding their little stoical horses. And quite looking forward to it all.

We are left with our lives, someone said to me. All the other stuff, the poisonous foreign stuff, the stuff that makes us jealous and empty, is being taken away and, like children when the toys have to go back in the box, we're feeling sorry for ourselves a little. But now we'll fish and cure mutton and make skyr (a particularly fine hybrid of cheese and yoghurt). You British have money, another older man said to me. You like it, you are comfortable with money. We weren't. All our history is the story of poor people surviving. We're good at that. There is a pride in that.

And there is a lesson here. While the rest of the world prints money to stave off the consequences of having spent too much, and borrows more to mitigate the borrowing, so the Icelanders are settling into their penury like men who've come back from a holiday slipping into their old threadbare coats, taking comfort in familiarity and pleasure in being relieved from avarice.

I drove out one night away from the city until all the terrestrial lights had vanished and there was only the great blackness and the pinpricked sky with its fluster of heavy cloud, and the ear-biting air was full of the chuffing wind and the shingly hiss of the shore, and the place was as full of ancient awe and keening sagas and bitter serenity as the end of the world.

There's no place like home

When it comes to humour and holidays, familiarity breeds contempt.

American newspapers have begun to cull comic strips.
Readers are being asked whether *Peanuts* or *Love Is...*
should get the comic cut. Don't all shout at once. America
invented the comic strip (as well as the crossword). In
fact, they invented the newsless newspaper. Most rags
have accumulated dozens of 'toons, sometimes as many as
four pages' worth. The reason for giving them the bullet/
falling piano/exploding cigar/sudden cliff/brick wall –
they say – is rising print costs and falling advertising. But
anyone who's travelled through the States recently will
have caught a sniff of the real reason, heard the warning
bark. America is losing its sense of humour.

Now, the American joke is rather like the American
car. It's big and comfortable and slow and oversprung. It's
probably got wings and it helps if you've drunk a lot. The
great American joke and its sister, the great American
dream, are confirmations of the greatness of America. The
specific content is not important – either of the joke or the
dream. It's having one and sharing that's American. And
it's gone. Or rather, it's become hard and brittle, bitter
and spit-flecked. The huge fraternity of the set-up and
the punchline has become the snarl and exhaust of the

bumper sticker. America is a fair-weather goodtime joker. It doesn't do what the rest of the world does, and laugh at adversity. America panics at adversity. It panics in slow motion with a straight face.

The airport thing is only the start. That dull, plodding suspicion, the zero-tolerance rigmarole of welcome that make you think that, having invented powered flight, the locals have come to regard it as a mechanism of the devil, dabbled in only by deviants and the combustible. It's not that all visitors are looking for auguries and visible symbols of wartime change in the States, it's that the Americans themselves are not just suspicious – they're superstitious-suspicious. A nation with so much faith, it doesn't know how to stop believing in things. This is not a time to make jokes; a joke can get you arrested, a joke can get you deported. This is a time to go and read your horoscope and look stern.

I've just been travelling through Maryland, a state that is a suburb of Washington, home to professional apparatchiks. It's where you park your porky backside if you have your nose in the trough. It's also got Baltimore, home of Francis Scott Key and the American national anthem, and Annapolis, the naval college, and Chesapeake Bay, and not much else. A border state between north and south siding, after much anguish, with Lincoln and the angels. It feels like the North. It doesn't have that foxy, inbred sense of danger and carnality you get in the South.

Mostly Maryland is a place beside the sea. You drive through the now-ubiquitous fields of corn – when did America decide to grow only one thing? – like a bushy yellow monobrow. At the roadside, farmyard stalls sell garden peaches, goitred, livid tomatoes and huge, husky heaps of sweet corn, but you sense that this is a place that farms backdrops and vistas for the serenity and cosy good nature of the four-wheel drive mums and weekend ruralists.

I was headed for Ocean City, a town on the sea. One of the obliquely good things about America is that outside of New York, nothing is designed, sold or made for foreign tourists. Foreigners aren't a market – they're a threat, or they're busboys. But then most Americans are tourists in their own country, so almost everywhere that has two diners and a local specialty has a big welcome for guests. Ocean City is built on a long spit of sand. These bars and slim islands run like morse code up the east coast, making some of the nicest seaside destinations on the Atlantic. Ocean City isn't one of them.

Ocean City is gaudily hellish. Three broad streets wide, and a hundred or so cross-streets long, it's a strip of economy high-rise hotels and greater-economy motels of the sort that make you think of suicides, underage sex and men who dress up as their mothers. These are interspersed by economy beachwear shops selling towelling shellsuits and novelty T-shirts, and all-you-can-eat restaurants and giveaway churches.

One of the other odd things about Americans is that they take so few holidays – and in such parsimonious increments. Families chug into Ocean City in desert-storming SUVs having driven across three states to spend a short weekend having economy fun. Everything needs to be accessible on an American holiday, so resorts come on naked, like strippers who haven't got time to strip. Americans approach beaches as if for the first time. Ocean City's beach is nothing to write home about, nothing to wish-you-were-here on. A long motorway of sand with a cold, grey aggressive Atlantic in front and the cold, grey passive hotels behind.

The families stagger with armfuls of paraphernalia,
like proud Cortés, coming upon the sea with an exhausted
yet wary awe. They sit on their fold-out chairs under their
fold-out umbrellas and hats and sunblock and suck a
litre of latte, eat a Danish or three, read a magazine. And
then they stare at the ocean, and the ocean ignores them,
so they stare at the lifeguards. There is a lifeguard on a
highchair every 20 yards (Ocean City has a museum to
lifeguarding). The lifeguards unpack their sunblock and
their hats and their rubber rings and their floats-on-ropes
and then they do semaphore to each other. Up and down
they wave their arms, like train signals in a gale. Who
knows what they're saying? 'Does my bum look big in
these?' perhaps.

When the holidaymakers have stopped looking at
the lifeguards they look at each other for a bit, and then
they stand up and get antsy. Something isn't happening.
Something is missing. Is there a show? Is there a band? Is
there lunch? A parade? Fireworks? Is there magic? When
does the beach do its thing? Americans are not good at
doing nothing. America wasn't built by people who could
do nothing with ease. It isn't a nation that relaxes, or
rewards relaxation. It's a get-up-and-go place, so they get
up and they go. They pack up their umbrellas and seats
and head back to the strip, where they play novelty golf.

I didn't mention the golf before because I was saving it.
I hate it so much. Ocean City has nine kids' golf courses.
Families come and play them like the majors, all in one
weekend. They start with the pirates and go through
the sci-fi monsters, then they do the dinosaurs and the
cowboys. They can't get enough of putting around corners.
And then they go and eat crab cakes and go back to their
hotel rooms and watch exactly the same television they get

back at home. And know that their towels won't be stolen
from the balcony railings. And I know what they're doing,
what America's doing. It's turning its back – turning its
back on everything.

They're coming here to play novelty golf and eat crab
cakes and stay in these hokey, tacky low-rent, low-crime
resorts because it reminds them of somewhere else.
Some place past. Some safe past place that you see in
pictures or glimpse in the afternoons on cable TV. There
are teenagers here, tough hip-hop, baggy, gangbanging
teenagers, queuing up for their putters and a ball because
everyone needs a weekend away from orange alerts and
politics and being frightened, even crack dealers and
car thieves. And if you can't laugh, at least you can get
nostalgic and buy a T-shirt with a flag on it.

When they asked the readers which comic strips they
should get rid of, they all chose the modern ones – the
sharp, sarky, ethnic, smart-arse ones. They wanted to
keep the strips they'd read all their lives – the old hokey
familiar ones. The ones that aren't funny.

Between the lines

----

*Mapmakers speak a language
of contours and borders, but
this lexicon says nothing of the
relationship between geography
and people. And they've missed
Greenland completely.*

What's the biggest island in the world? If you answered,
Australia, you effete pommy know-all, well I'm sorry
– go and face the wall by the nature table. If you said
Tasmania, go and sit on the nature table. Australia is
a continent and therefore doesn't count as an island,
and if continents were eligible as islands, then America
would be the biggest. The biggest island in the world is
Greenland, which makes Denmark the biggest country in
Europe, because Denmark owns Greenland. Except that
it isn't, because geographically Greenland is part of
North America. It's separated from Canada by about as
far as an angry girlfriend can throw your copy of *Call of
the Wild*.

I've just returned from East Greenland, and there's not
a lot of people for whom that proximity is a reality. Even
for most of the people in West Greenland it is cheaper
to fly from East Greenland to Reykjavik and then on to
New York than to fly across the country. It's that big. It's
four time zones, without a single clock in two of them.
Greenland is twice the size of the next biggest island,

which is either Borneo, Madagascar or New Guinea. Well
done those of you who said New Guinea.

It makes you think a lot about whether size matters.
Despite its massive size, Greenland barely registers a blip
on the world political, economic or social consciousness.
In fact, none of the top four big islands are exactly what
you'd call movers or shakers. On most maps, Greenland
is shoved to one side or cut in half, effectively squeezed
to the edge of the world. Indeed, being up there in the
permanent daylight it feels like the edge of the world.

Geography is all about size. Kids who like geography
in school are the ones who like lists, like to know the
heft and the girth of things. I liked geography. The
hottest place in the world? The record temperature is
in the Libyan desert, though it might be Ethiopia. The
coldest? Lived-in or uninhabited? Uninhabited, the
South Pole. Inhabited, Greenland, where there is a dry
wind that comes off the ice cap and blows harder than a
hurricane. God knows what its wind-chill factor is. The
wettest place, the driest, the highest capital? That would
be Lima, wouldn't it, or perhaps La Paz? Capital furthest
north? That's Reykjavik. Rivers, mountains, basins,
plains, plateaux, distances. We keep on and on trying to
understand the globe by its statistics, by its facts, but
really it's like trying to know a stranger by his laundry list.

Size has another effect on people. In Greenland, the
Inuit only live at the very edge of the country. In 4000
years, they've ebbed and flowed up and down its vastness,
but haven't ever really got off the beach. You feel all
this great empty howling, keening space stretching away
behind you, the infeasible, unimaginable pristine freezing
whiteness. There's a similar sense in Brazil. Again, almost
everyone lives on the coast; behind them the steaming,

dripping green and fetid dense land, lurking with not entirely loving attention.

Size intimidates, and it informs the national character. Though Inuits and Brazilians couldn't be more unalike, they're both people who are made by their landscapes. Now coming from a relatively small island such as Britain or Japan, or indeed Iceland, gives you a very different sense of who you are. We make the landscape in our own image. It's a tame and malleable place. Our geography is raw material; it's a stroll, a hike, a summer holiday. We think of the world as being an eventually manageable benign place. We come from humanised, human-sized countries.

There are people who are inspired by the size of their countries, like Americans. That ability to pick up sticks and start all over is central to Americans' idea of themselves. The open road, the new horizon, the ripe and unending bounty of the country. Then there are people who are confined by their geography, who will feel crowded and claustrophobic. The Swiss, the Cubans. Always looking over the fence. King Leopold bought the Congo specifically because he despised the small-town, little-nation bourgeois beer-and-chocolate mentality of his Belgian subjects. He felt that they could do with getting out a bit more. The Russians all need to get out a bit more, and then when they do, you wish they'd all go back.

Maps don't tell you the things that would be really useful to know about the world. The most boring place, for instance – East Germany. The rudest? Israel. The best-looking men? Cuba. And women? Somalia and Uzbekistan. The best breakfast? Paris and Hanoi. The best lunch? Sicily and Belgium. The best dinner? Bombay and Singapore. Maps should also tell you the most optimistic landscapes, and the most depressing. More of the world

is on the move now than in any time since the fall of the
Roman Empire. Millions and millions of slow unromantic
odysseys, looking for something, for safety, for opportunity,
a wife, a tan, a thrill, a chance, a decent night's sleep.
How we see a journey is not measured by where we think
we'll end up, but from where we start off.

Maps are static things. Greenland is the only place
in the world that is uncharted. Look at it: it's an outline
with a blank white interior. No one has ever made a map
of it, no one's been to mark its contours and ravines, its
plains or its peaks. It is the most spectacular landscape
I've seen for a long time. The air is so clear you can see
for hundreds of kilometres, and it's not mapped because
there's no point to mapping it. Nothing lives in the middle.
Nothing survives there. A map is a diagram of interest
and expectation. And there is none in Greenland, and that
makes it extraordinary.

The anonymous white, the enormous white is the
world's largest lump of ice, the world's biggest, greatest
reserve of water. And it's melting. Last year the pack-ice
wasn't thick enough to take the weight of the sleds and the
Inuits' dogs starved. When the ice all melts, it will re-draw
the map of the world. Countries will vanish, cities drown,
borders will be meaningless. Every atlas and globe that
has been settled for a thousand years will be obsolete. And
a country that no one ever thinks of, that barely makes it
to the back of the picture, will have redrawn the world.

Head space

The world we imagine is almost always different to the reality, and our grand imaginings of destinations inevitably affect the experience.

Every place is three places. A trinity, separate but indivisible. A place is first the place you imagine, then the place you see, and then finally the place you remember. They are all distinct, they're related, all different, though none of them remain the same. The place you imagined is changed by the place you see, and that in turn changes as everywhere does. And memory is as ethereal as a performance that alters with every retelling. This all may seem a little esoteric, a little French-drawing-room, but I've been thinking about it because I'm going back to Haiti.

The world we imagine, we remember, is seen in a circus mirror. Whole continents shrink to mere specks. Some places are just blurred outlines, others grow disproportionately large. The centre of the universe may be a random but memorable city: the place of your birth, somewhere you were happy, where your family emigrated from, like those Dark Ages maps where the world revolves around Jerusalem. And there are fanciful lands full of monsters and misbegotten beasts. And that's what I feel about Haiti. In my personal topography, it's vast, a huge place inhabited by mythological creatures and fierce folk. When I finally walked across the tarmac to leave Port-au-Prince, I realised I'd spent a week with hunched shoulders expecting a blow. I have never before or since had the physical experience of a weight being lifted from my shoulders, and as I stepped onto the plane, I said, 'Thank God, I'll never have to come back here again.' You should not only be careful what you pray for, but about what you're thankful for.

I imagined Haiti as a darker Caribbean island, a mixture of James Bond and Graham Greene. It was so much more compellingly grim than that, more frightening, an example of what destitution, despair and hysterical imaginations can conjure up. Imagine John the Divine crossed with Keyser Söze crossed with the man pushing the shopping trolley who shouts at the traffic, and that's how I remember Haiti. Now, of course, the reality has been severely challenged by tectonic plates. Although I found the time I spent in Port-au-Prince testing and mostly terrifying, it's remained with me, loomed large in the reverie of my bespoke world. I can conjure up the smells, the men with yellow eyes, the hymn-singing from high windows, the shrieks that came out of the dark. It proves a glib travellers' rule that the places that stay with you, that are the most memorable, are rarely the most pleasant.

This brings me to space. Because whilst I was having my anxiety attack about going back to Haiti, I also considered going to the moon because someone had just told me that Buzz Aldrin – the Buzz Aldrin – is going to be doing a reality show on TV about dancing. It doesn't matter whether this is a real show or if it's the real Buzz

Aldrin – the point is it could be; I believe it is. You could believe that Buzz Aldrin was going to do a reality show about dancing and then fall on his arse in a flamenco shirt. This is how we will remember the second man who ever stepped onto the moon.

Space travel has been promised as a tourist destination for about 20 years, but apart from a couple of American millionaires, it hasn't happened. Virgin Galactic is still taking bookings for passengers for the destination with less atmosphere than Starbucks. Soon, they'll be asking journalists to go on freebies, and I'm thinking, would I rather go to Haiti or into orbit with five American millionaires whose favourite film is *The Right Stuff* and who all want to be Chuck Yeager?

But I think space has missed the boat, or perhaps the rocket. Nothing has been as downgraded in the collective imagination as astronauts. In the '60s, they were the apogee of human achievement. Spacemen embodied everything we aspired to as a species. If you viewed natural selection as a pyramid with the Welsh at the bottom, the pointy stone at the top was a man wearing a fish tank on his head. Today an astronaut is a Russian plumber who's gone into orbit to mend the air-conditioning or to unblock the gravity-dunny. When was the last time you knew the name of a spaceman? (And we're not counting Buzz Lightyear.)

The space station looks like a postgraduate student hostel. Now that NASA has been told it's not going anywhere and its role will be to train pilots to give tours around guided-launch sites to a diminishing band of science-fiction nerds, space has become the great disappointment of our time. It embodied so much; it was all so rich in metaphor.

I went to the Museum of Cosmonautics in Moscow
once. It was virtually empty except for a few dissolute
schoolkids being prodded around by physics teachers.
It's not popular in Russia now; too redolent of old red-
faced communists. The rockets and the silver suits look
like bad props from cheap movies. The one thing that
grabbed my attention was a tiny Sputnik that had taken
Laika the dog into space. It wasn't the original, of course.
That, unlike Lassie, never came home. There was a stuffed
dog strapped into the replica, and I wondered at the very
Dostoevskian irony of one dog being condemned to death
by being sent into the great never-never, and another one
murdered to represent the first one when it was alive.

The problem with space was that the trinity of places
didn't obey the terrestrial rules. The imagined place was
so grand, so replete with expectation and fiction that
the real place couldn't compete. Indeed, the real place
turned out to be no place at all. And the memories that
came back from it were so mundane, so weird, so middle
American, so earthbound that before we ever took off it
became dull and suburban, full of second-hand satellites
and GPS signals, a junk-lot of ugly bits of silver stuff.
We ruined it without ever having gone there. The abiding
memory of space may be of old Buzz gliding along on one
arthritic leg, arms outstretched, to the sound of 'Thus
Spoke Zarathustra', to obscurity and beyond.

The fall of summer

It's always summer that gets the girl and has the time of its life. But autumn, especially in the beautiful countryside of northern England, has charms of its own.

One of the rarely mentioned but horribly inequitable truths of life is that the rich not only live longer than the rest of us, but they get more summers. For you and I, summers come but once a year, and often, up here in Blighty, it doesn't even come then. But for the leisured and sybaritic, they can have as many as two or three summers in a year. I've known men whose entire lives have been one long summer. They savour bits of their own and then take bits of other people's around the world. It should be possible to work out a global itinerary where you can keep travelling elliptically north-west to south-east forever running between the solstices. Solsterie. Solstercii.

Most people who travel occasionally only know the world in brightness and warmth. Of all the seasons, summer has the best PR, gets all the glossy spreads and the lounging bikini shots. It's always summer that gets the girl and has the time of its life. Summer is the Marilyn Monroe of the seasons. The hot good time that is had by all and ends in tears.

But if you travel in the heat and the bright, you miss a lot of the subtlety of the world.

Northern Europe is marvellous in the winter. The smell of cloves and hot wine, cinnamon and chocolate, the glow of candles, the ancient festivals and feasts, velvet and fur. And everyone should experience one monsoon in their lives. The heavy, hot, humid expectation of rain, the teasing dry thunder, the clouds gathering and then the downpour, the refreshing, rehydrating release of it. And you should see the desert after it rains to realise the tenacity and patience of nature's optimism.

Here, at home in England, my favourite season isn't summer, which is mostly a chilly drizzling disappointment, a test of the water-resistance of platitudes, cream teas and the transparency of soaked summer frocks. Summer in England, with all its mythologised bee-humming somnambulant village-cricket-on-the-green resonances is mostly a creation of nostalgia. Stories that start, 'It was one of those glorious summer days ...' Glorious summer days are miraculous things, and memories are often transported to them retrospectively to add lustre.

My favourite season is autumn. This century is being blessed with exceptional autumns. It may be a dividend of global warming. Country men, those perennial weather-bores, stand on gates and say, 'The hornbeam has never been this late, we haven't had a decent frost yet, the chaffinches are still in the ash.' There are still unicorns in the top pasture and the mute swans are talking gibberish. And it's already November. Country lore is all about things going wrong or being dead or barren. But the trees have grown New World-gaudy. The hedgerows are heavy with rowans and sloes. The mildness of the season means that some of the greenery hangs on to the very last. A rose in my garden bursts a final bloom of white, like the ultimate shot of summer's ack-ack.

Autumn's the time I like to go to the countryside. In fact, it's the only time I can abide the countryside. It smells differently now, ripe and juicy, the scent of fresh rot and leaf mulch, fox piss and wood smoke. There are mushrooms in the oak woods, chanterelles and cepes pushing through the mould. The mornings are hooded in mists that make the coppices and woods look like green islands in a white sea. Sodden straggling sheep chew over harvested fields. The scent of turned earth and straw. The light slants at you sideways, shredded into filigree patterns by the branches of beeches and chestnuts. The air is the colour of weak tea. Autumn is particularly good because not only is the country dressed for the weather, but so can you be. Summer is so unflattering for men over 30. Far better to wear tweed and corduroy, leather and stout boots.

I've just come back from Northumberland, the most northerly and one of the least-visited counties in England. And possibly my favourite. Its next-door neighbour, Cumbria, gets all the plaudits and poems, containing as it does the Lake District, with its maudlin doggerel and obsessive-depressive hikers. Cumbria is a steady stream of Bri-Nylon hill-walkers, cloudy-breathed and bandy-legged, looking for tea shops run by lost hippies.

Northumberland has none of that. It's a tightly inverted place with few tourist attractions. There's the scar of Hadrian's Wall, a few squat market towns like Hexham, the border city of Berwick-upon-Tweed that used to be the second most populous in Scotland before it was annexed by Edward I as a staging post for his invasions (although technically it's English, its football team is in the Scottish league). It has a feeling of a place apart, sitting behind Tudor battlements waiting for the worst. There is the great

spine of the Cheviot Hills that marks the border with
Scotland, bruised with heather and green granite, dusted
with snow before the rest of the country has picked its last
apples or put on its central heating.

And there is the coast that only a drunk teenager, a
seal or a labrador would swim in, that is one of the most
searingly beautiful stretches of shore in Europe. Ruffled
and salt-scarred, it has the great castles of Bamburgh and
Alnwick and the magic, holy island Lindisfarne, where
Christianity clung to northern Europe during the Dark
Ages, a little glinting gleam that sheltered Bede and
the Pentecostally inspired illuminators of gospels. This
was the coast that the Viking longships most commonly
raided, and Northumberland became the heart of a Viking
kingdom. The people here still talk with a rolling semi-
Scandinavian lilt and have the look of rape and pillage
about them.

This was always a hard place. After the Vikings, it
had three centuries of border wars. Northumberland was
constantly at feud with its neighbours in the lowlands.
The battles were vicious, the memories long and the
mutual impoverishment of the border debilitating, even
to this day. Northumberland lacks the manor houses and
rich farms that spread through the rest of England after
the Tudors. Here, there are the stumpy remains of peel
towers, plain defensive forts. It has a broad, hard, rolling
landscape that's the perfect evocation of its mystical and
murderous history. People here don't move around much
– they stick close to the land, and they treat it and curse
it with a tough love for a small living. Autumn is a perfect
time to see Northumberland. And last weekend was one of
those glorious autumn days.

Extreme of consciousness

One day a refugee camp, the next a South-of-France soiree ... true extreme travel is not remote and dangerous places, but the juxtaposition of opposites.

Chad, a land where the sun doesn't just shine, it polishes and scrubs until you feel like a gay gardener's fly button. Chad, where a thin stick's shadow counts as air-conditioning, where you can fry an egg on the Land Rover bonnet – in the middle of the night. Chad, where you don't sweat and you don't pee, you just evaporate. I've been to some hot places, and in general I don't mind. It's certainly preferable to the alternative. But the heat in Chad is something else: 34°C in the shade at 6am.

You get the feeling that Chad is only a country because cartographers, like quilt makers, can't abide gaps. It's essentially somewhere to put the right-hand corner of the Sahara, and to stop Libya slipping into Nigeria. The capital, N'Djamena, has an airport. It has an airport to make itself feel like a destination. For some fathomless reason, aeroplanes seem to think it's a destination, too. It's a two-storey place of whitewashed breeze-block, barbed-wire, filigreed shade trees and dusty dogs who are all cousins.

It's tough travelling in Chad. You either drive in the bucking, tyre-sucking mine-strewn roads in a bread-oven Toyota or you fly. To fly, you have to beg a ride from the United Nations or a charity. Getting charity from a charity is tough. You get bumped off. And that means you can get left for a week in some place so bereft it doesn't even have flies.

I was here to cover a story about refugees from a nasty genocidal war being waged across the border in Sudan. You don't feel like eating much in a refugee camp, even when there is something to eat. But after 10 days of tepid, sulky water and melted chewing gum, you begin to feel like you're self-ingesting.

I was lying one sweltering night under a mosquito net up against a mud wall watching the shooting stars spin past a minaret of a distant mosque. We were right on the border with Sudan, over a dry stream. The other half of the town lay deserted, pockmarked in the silver light.

'If you could eat anything, what would it be right now?' asked the photographer. Oh, don't start with the last-orders desert-island stuff. It just makes you miserable and ravenous. I haven't thought about food for days. 'Yeah, but what would it be?' I closed my eyes and saw, smelt, touched and tasted two soft-boiled eggs in a blue-and-white eggcup. A baguette with pale white, sweet, cool butter and runny wild-strawberry jam. A bowl of coffee with just a touch of chicory. A jug of hot milk. I could feel the thick napkin and smell the early-morning lavender.

Now, I've often played 'My Favourite Meal', and over the years it's evolved into quite an elaborate repast, demanding a number of chefs, an epicurean treasure-trove of ingredients and a platoon of staff to prepare and serve. I never imagined that when the chips were down, so to speak, I'd conjure up a continental breakfast. 'What would you have?' I asked the snapper. 'Oh, I'll have what you're having. Order two. Tell room service to mind the goats. And to bring some ice – I'd like some ice.'

We did the story. We toured the camps and the therapeutic feeding centres for the tiny children that lie, listless with wide eyes, too exhausted to cry, and we started to make the long trip back to N'Djamena, getting to a French Foreign Legion airbase to catch a UN flight.

Nervously, I waited for the fixer to allot our seats. Just as we were about to get on, a Jeep spun up with an immaculate government minister in it. He stepped out with a French paratrooper escort. He's going to nick my seat. Then behind him a pick-up arrived, and in the back of the pick-up was a crate, and in the crate, nearly head high, was a lady ostrich.

The captain, a Dane in Ray-Bans, took one chilly Nordic look and said, 'The ostrich is a flightless bird.' I bounded up the steps and strapped myself in. The minister bumped out a relief nurse who'd just spent three months in an emergency hospital and had a weekend's leave, and we taxied off. I watched the paratrooper, eyes slitted against the prop dust, standing beside the ostrich in a box. They both looked mightily pissed off.

That night I sat drinking warm Coke in the blacked-out international airport, crossing and uncrossing my fingers for the flight to Paris. In Paris, I ran through terminals to jump a flight to Nice. In Nice, I was picked up by a limo and driven to a villa on the tip of St Tropez. In the villa was my girlfriend. 'Sit here in the garden,' she said. 'You must be hungry.'

I sat and looked out over the chickens and the orchard and the vineyard and the great, cantilevered parapluie pines, down across the fields full of wildflowers and out to sea. I was still in the clothes I'd travelled in. My bush jacket stiff with Africa. My hair thick with Africa. My new beard smelling of Africa. And there were two soft-boiled eggs – and you know the rest.

It was all exactly as I'd imagined it, right down to the whisper of chicory in the coffee. It was one of those small moments of connectedness that have a monumental significance. It's difficult to explain, but I felt like time had been threaded through the eye of a needle. It was a moment when the fact lived up to the expectation.

That night I ate in one of my favourite restaurants in the world, the Auberge de la Mole in the hills above St Tropez. Rillettes and pâté, intense little cornichons. Delectable frogs' legs kicking in butter and garlic. A tournedos Rossini with a duvet of thick foie gras. Finely sliced waxy potatoes baked duck fat-crisp in a timbale. Perfect roquefort and a sweet French snog of a dribbling crème brûlée. That's an almost perfect menu.

The next day we went along the coast to the Cap d'Antibes and a yacht moored off the Eden-Roc Hotel for Vanity Fair's Cannes film festival party. It was extreme. The distance between Chad and Antibes is about as radical as you could arrange in this world, and actually the combination was immensely invigorating. I rather thought that I'd suffer from whingeing culture shock and get all sulky about the conspicuous consumption and the vanity of Vanity Fair and Hollywood sur-la-mer. But, actually, I really adored it.

In previous years I've affected a blasé ennui, but a week in a desert refugee camp makes you realise nothing can be taken for granted, and the sin of luxury is not in the thing itself but in failing to appreciate it. That's not trite – well, it is trite, but it doesn't stop it being true. True extreme travel is not remote and dangerous places, but the juxtaposition of opposites.

I'm going to start doing binary shock holidays. Havana, then Reykjavik. Cairo, then South Georgia. The Vatican, then Easter Island. It doesn't even have to be expensive or difficult. You could work out an extreme binary day break, such as a lap-dancing lunch and then your mother-in-law's for dinner.

Terminal love

In the arrivals hall, it's hard not to be moved by the great black lake of tears that immigration leaves behind.

Airports. You've got to love them. No, really. You have got to love them. At least, you must learn to appreciate them. If you don't, life will be a constant dung sarnie of places you want to be sandwiched between termini of frustration and worry, boredom and fury.

I get on with airports. I like the way they look. I appreciate their ergonomics, their thousands of moving parts, the ant-hill logistics of getting everything in and out. You couldn't have come up with something more complicated, thousands of people separated from thousands of pieces of luggage, having to be in a certain seat at a precise time to go up to hundreds of destinations. Add thousands of bits of separated luggage and their people coming the other way, all speaking different languages, some travelling for the first time, some for the umpteenth. And just to make it all more exciting, you have to assume that any one of them might be a self-martyring mass murderer and that they will all want to spend 10 pounds on something they didn't know they needed, and a penny, which they probably suspected they would need.

My love of airports is based on going somewhere, or coming back from somewhere. I'm rarely in airports for any other reason. But last week, I went to Gatwick to meet my daughter. I can't remember the last time I met someone at an airport or indeed was met by anyone who wasn't a driver. But part of the drama of an airport is walking through the exit at the arrivals lounge, the anxiety of luggage and passports and customs behind you, and that audience expectant and attentive. You move through the door, humping your rucksack, rumpled from the flight, still smelling of air freshener and with bits of exploding bread rolls collected in the folds of your sticky shirt and suddenly you're on stage. For a fleeting moment, you think that maybe, just perhaps, there will be someone here for you.

This is an intense and fraught stage, live with expectation, and among the lounging, bored drivers with their scrawled cardboard signs of misspelt names and company logos, there are also the worried faces of family, friends. And as you slide past them, you can see little narratives: a woman waiting for a man she fell in love with over the internet and has never met, an immigrant's child finally given a visa, the divorced parent coming for a brief summer holiday – all the gossamer loose ends of human relationships waiting to be tied up in this concourse.

It's the constant darning of the oldest plot in the world: departures and arrivals, the most ancient saga of travelling and returning. You realise that leaving your clan, your protective family group, is fraught. Our natural genetic impulse is to stay close: our history, our tribal instinct, pulls us back together. Our emotions twist the pressure with homesickness and longing, missing the taste of familiar food, the smell of childhood. All that nostalgia, that awkward nag of belonging, the tug of home, all tell us where we should be.

Still, there is also that itch and excitement of getting away, the adventure, the experience. These are contradictory human urges that are all exposed in the airport. And I'm not used to being here as a non-traveller. I haven't seen Flora for five months. This is the longest absence in her whole 19 years of life, this gap-year thing that is peculiarly Anglo-Saxon. Australians do it all the time, being caught at the far distant end of Europe's elastic. Every autumn thousands of middle-class kids finish their A-levels, work for a few months and then, in threes and fours, wander out into the world.

What surprised me was my reaction to Flora going. I've always encouraged my children to be inquisitive, to get out there, to see the world. We only pass this way once, I tell them, this globe is where you live, not just this corner of this one city. See your birthright, meet the neighbours, don't just leave your travelling to the TV and glossy magazines. There've always been maps in their rooms and travellers' tales on their bookshelves. When Flora finally hefted my old rucksack and left, I was completely unnerved by it, irritated that she was so insouciant about the journey, so candidly trusting in the goodness of the world, that it would all be all right. I became peevish and nagging with warnings and fears about mosquitoes and bed bugs, mopeds, footpads, jellyfish and amoeba, money belts and etiquette. She was smilingly oblivious and disappeared into the great migration of public school teenagers slogging around the Far East for full-moon parties, inner-tube floating, 12-hour bus rides, huts on beaches, buckets of Red Bull and vodka, flaming limbo dancing, DayGlo face paint and tattoos.

What I felt was the old Velcro rip of affection and connection. My old bore's experienced cautionary

instructions were really just displacement for a siren of
worry and sadness about the passing of childhood. Of
course, it was only a holiday. How much worse would
migrating have been? For the past 200 years, so much
of Europe moved away. Now, even you at the end of the
world, you're as close as a computer screen or a phone
in your pocket. But in the '60s when the 10-pound
Poms arrived, their families must have known that the
likelihood was that they'd be able to count the number of
times they'd see them again on the fingers of one hand –
possibly never.

I've been writing a lot about migration recently. And
I'm aware of the great black mere of tears that immigration
leaves behind, the terrible mourning and loss and the
sadness of economic and political migrants. It marks
countries. It marked Ireland and Scotland and it's marked
many others. We rarely notice or acknowledge that the
greatest gift of being members of the First World club is
that we can afford to stay close to our parents and our
children and that we can travel with the comfort and
assurance of knowing we can get back from anywhere
within 24 hours.

While I waited for Flora at the arrivals, I was surprised
by the depth and the sharpness of my own anticipation,
how much I'd missed her. I watched a trickle of travellers
returning. In front of me were a huddle of family: a father
and mother and a couple of boys. They were subdued;
they had been waiting some time. The children were
bored and unhappy, the man kept a protective arm around
his wife. Then in through the doors came a woman with
a small hurried bag. She was plainly the wife's sister. A
called name and the two women ran towards each other
and hugged and the connection, the touch, unlocked a

dam of tears and they sagged into each other's shoulders
and sobbed. The father and children hung back. Without
words, you knew that a parent had died. That the
immigrant child was returning for the funeral too late
to say goodbye or thank you. And as they moved slowly
towards the exit, there was a shrill call of 'Daddy!' and
Flora in crumpled brightly tie-dyed cotton, with matted
hair and barnacled with bangles, dropped her bag and ran
to the barrier, a grin like a sickle moon, relieved, I think,
to find that I was still here with the living and that, finally,
there was someone else to carry her rucksack.

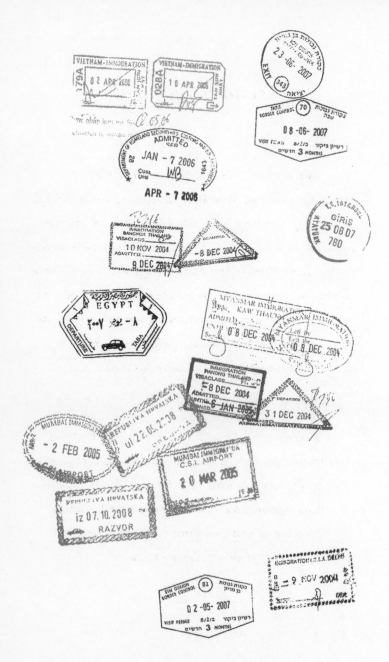

Acknowledgements

Firstly I must thank Anthea, the Editor of
Australian Gourmet Traveller, *for inviting me to write for*
her magazine, and then putting up with my writing,
particularly the firm but fair things I've occasionally had
to say about Greeks. And I owe a huge debt of gratitude
to Pat Nourse, who has chased me for copy, recorded my
sleepy, ungrammatical rants and turned them into the
glowing pearls you now hold in your hand,
without ever once losing his temper.

The pleasure of the craft of journalism is that you
start to work for money, but end up working with friends,
and collaborating with Pat's humour, erudition and
encouragement on these essays has made them a
pleasure to write, and this collection a source
of pride and happy memory.

Published in 2011 by Hardie Grant Books

Hardie Grant Books (Australia)
85 High Street
Prahran, Victoria 3181
www.hardiegrant.com.au

Hardie Grant Books (UK)
Second Floor, North Suite
Dudley House
Southampton Street
London WC2E 7HF
www.hardiegrant.co.uk

National Library of Australia Cataloguing-in-Publication data
Author: Gill, A. A.
Title: Here and there : collected travel writing / A A Gill.
ISBN: 9781742701622 (pbk.)
Subjects: Gill, A. A. Travel. Voyages and travels. Tourism and gastronomy.
Dewey Number: 790.18

Publisher: Paul McNally
Project editor: Jane Winning
Cover design: Design by Committee
Internal design: Heather Menzies
Typesetting: Pauline Haas
Colour reproduction by Splitting Image Colour Studio
Printed in Australia by Griffin Press